SOUTH-WESTERN

C++
Programming Projects
ACTIVITIES WORKBOOK

CEP, Inc.

John Sestak

VISIT US ON THE INTERNET
www.swep.com

South-Western Educational Publishing
an International Thomson Publishing company I(T)P®
www.thomson.com

Cincinnati • Albany, NY • Belmont, CA • Bonn • Boston • Detroit • Johannesburg • London • Madrid
Melbourne • Mexico City • New York • Paris • Singapore • Tokyo • Toronto • Washington

Library of Congress Cataloging-in-Publication Data
Sestak, John.
    C++ programming projects / John Sestak.
        p. cm.
    Includes index.
    ISBN 0-538-69081-X
    1. C++ (Computer program language)   I. Title.
QA76.73.C153S385   2000
005.13'3—dc21

99-12330
CIP

Managing Editor: Carol Volz
Production Manager: Dave Lafferty
Consulting Editor: Custom Editorial Productions, Inc.
Marketing Manager: Larry Qualls
Design Coordinator: Mike Broussard
Production: Custom Editorial Productions, Inc.

Copyright © 2000
By SOUTH-WESTERN EDUCATIONAL PUBLISHING
Cincinnati, Ohio

ISBN: 0-538-69081-X

1 2 3 4 5 WE 02 01 00 99

Printed in the United States of America

I(T)P®

International Thomson Publishing

South-Western Educational Publishing is a division of International Thomson Publishing, Inc. The ITP registered
trademark is used under license.

PREFACE

The purpose of this project book is to reinforce the topics that you have been exposed to in your C++ class. It is intended to support the textbook from which you have been learning theory. The projects in this book are "C++ oriented," meaning each program should run on any compiler. There are no specific code sequences that are meant to be run on one compiler. Programming expertise comes from using the materials that have been presented to you over and over again. The old adage, "practice makes perfect," definitely holds true when dealing with programming. And that is the purpose of this project book—to give you the opportunity to practice, practice, practice!

Using This Book

The programs you develop in this book will work whether you are using Visual C++ 6.0, an earlier version of it, or a simple text editor.

Each project and end-of-lesson application is identified as either a beginner (B), intermediate (I), or advanced (A) level activity. You will also notice that some exercises are marked with a SCANS icon. SCANS stands for the Secretary's Commission on Achieving Necessary Skills. A SCANS icon next to an exercise indicates that it satisfies a majority of the workplace competency and foundation skills identified by the commission.

This book is accompanied by the *Electronic Instructor* CD. This invaluable resource contains printouts of the code for each program you create, answers to project and end-of-lesson Review Questions, and other components designed to enhance the learning experience.

Acknowledgments

I would like to thank God for providing me with the ability to share my knowledge with others. I would like to thank Todd Knowlton for his recommendation, Dr. Ashraf Saad at the University of Cincinnati for his insightful review of the manuscript, and Tom Bockerstette for his thorough technical review. I'd like to thank Betsy Newberry, Laura Citro, and the rest of the staff at Custom Editorial Productions, Inc., and South-Western Educational Publishing for their belief in my ability to actually create this book. I would like to thank the students in my C++ class for using this material to reinforce my teaching. And, I would like to thank Tom Roncevic and Kyle Griffin, fellow instructors, for insights provided through various discussions.

Last, but certainly not least, I would like to thank my wife, Trish, and our three rugrats, Ryan, Kristi, and Tim, for working with me—and around me—as this book developed. I would also like to add my thanks to my mom and dad, who keep involved with everything I do. You realize that accomplishments become more meaningful when you have family that you can share them with.

John Sestak
Microsoft Certified Professional
Professional Trainer & Consultant
jsestak@pathway.net

How to Use this Text

What makes a good computer programming text? Sound pedagogy and the most current, complete materials. That is what you will find in the new *C++ Programming Projects*. Not only will you find an inviting layout, but also many features to enhance learning.

Objectives— Objectives are listed at the beginning of each lesson, along with a suggested time for completion of the lesson. This allows you to look ahead to what you will be learning and to pace your work.

Program Code Examples—Many examples of program code are included in the text to illustrate concepts under discussion.

Projects—Projects present hands on application of programming concepts and show the analysis, design, and implementation stages of the software development life cycle.

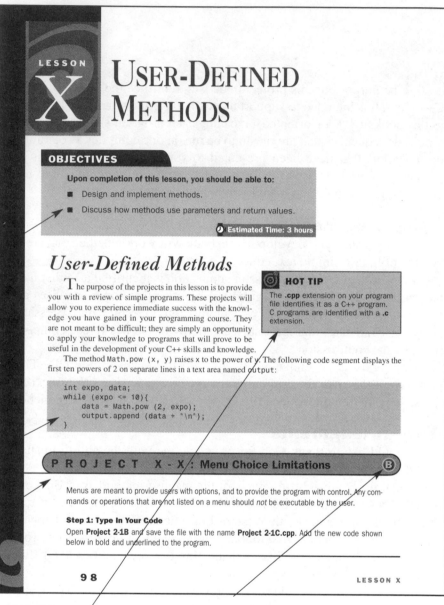

LESSON

X

USER-DEFINED METHODS

OBJECTIVES

Upon completion of this lesson, you should be able to:

- Design and implement methods.
- Discuss how methods use parameters and return values.

⏱ **Estimated Time: 3 hours**

User-Defined Methods

The purpose of the projects in this lesson is to provide you with a review of simple programs. These projects will allow you to experience immediate success with the knowledge you have gained in your programming course. They are not meant to be difficult; they are simply an opportunity to apply your knowledge to programs that will prove to be useful in the development of your C++ skills and knowledge.

The method Math.pow (x, y) raises x to the power of y. The following code segment displays the first ten powers of 2 on separate lines in a text area named output:

```
int expo, data;
while (expo <= 10){
    data = Math.pow (2, expo);
    output.append (data + "\n");
}
```

HOT TIP

The **.cpp** extension on your program file identifies it as a C++ program. C programs are identified with a **.c** extension.

PROJECT X - X : Menu Choice Limitations Ⓑ

Menus are meant to provide users with options, and to provide the program with control. Any commands or operations that are not listed on a menu should *not* be executable by the user.

Step 1: Type In Your Code

Open **Project 2-1B** and save the file with the name **Project 2-1C.cpp**. Add the new code shown below in bold and underlined to the program.

9 8

LESSON X

Hot Tip—These boxes provide enrichment information about C++.

Skill Level Icons— Each project and end-of-lesson activity is identified as either a beginner (B), intermediate (I), or advanced (A) level exercise.

How to Use this Text

Summary—At the end of each lesson, you will find a summary to help you complete the end-of-lesson activities.

Review Questions— Review material at the end of each lesson and each unit enables you to prepare for assessment of the content presented.

SCANS (Secretary's Commission on Achieving Necessary Skills)—The U.S. Department of Labor has identified the school-to-careers competencies. The five workplace competencies (resources, interpersonal skills, information, systems, and technology) and foundation skills (basic skills, thinking skills, and personal qualities) are identified in Projects and end-of-lesson activities throughout the text. More information on SCANS can be found on the *Electronic Instructor*.

Summary

In this lesson, you learned:

- The modern computer age began in the late 1940s with the development of ENIAC. Business computing became practical in the 1950s, and time-sharing computers advanced computing in large organizations in the 1960s.

LESSON X REVIEW QUESTIONS

SCANS

WRITTEN QUESTIONS

Write your answers to the following questions.

1. What are the three major hardware components of a computer?
2. Name three input devices.

TESTING YOUR SKILLS

Estimated Time:
Application 1-1 30 minutes
Application 1-2 30 minutes
Application 1-3 30 minutes

APPLICATION X-X

1. Add code to Project 1-1 that converts kilometers into miles.
   a. Open the **Project 1-1** program file.
   b. After the code that creates the output of the miles to kilometers conversion, add the necessary lines to perform a kilometers to miles conversion. The lines of code should be similar to the code used for the original program.

   HINT: The conversion this time is going in reverse. Use your algebra skills!

   c. Save your revised program as **App1-1**.

CRITICAL THINKING Ⓐ

Estimated Time: 1 hour

You have an idea for a program that will help the local pizza shop handle take-out orders. Your friend suggests an interview with the shop's owner to discuss her user requirements before you get started on the program. Explain why this is a good suggestion, and list the questions you would ask the owner to help you determine the user requirements.

9 9

Testing Your Skills— End-of-lesson hands-on application of what has been learned in the lesson allows you to actually apply the techniques covered.

Critical Thinking Activity—Each lesson gives you an opportunity to apply creative analysis to situations presented.

CONTENTS

1   Lesson 1: Simple Programs

Objectives   1
Introduction   1
Summary   9
Lesson 1 Review Questions   9
Testing Your Skills   11

13   Lesson 2: User Interaction

Objectives   13
Introduction   13
Summary   29
Lesson 2 Review Questions   30
Testing Your Skills   32

35   Lesson 3: Calculations

Objectives   35
Introduction   35
Summary   58
Lesson 3 Review Questions   59
Testing Your Skills   62

65   Lesson 4: Decision Making

Objectives   65
Introduction   65
Summary   92
Lesson 4 Review Questions   92
Testing Your Skills   95

99   Lesson 5: Repetitions

Objectives   99
Introduction   99
Summary   124
Lesson 5 Review Questions   124
Testing Your Skills   127

129   Lesson 6: Multiple Functions

Objectives   129
Introduction   129

Summary   157
Lesson 6 Review Questions   157
Testing Your Skills   160

163   Lesson 7: Basic Data Manipulation

Objectives   163
Introduction   163
Summary   185
Lesson 7 Review Questions   185
Testing Your Skills   189

191   Lesson 8: Simple Data Structures

Objectives   191
Introduction   191
Summary   209
Lesson 8 Review Questions   209
Testing Your Skills   212

213   Lesson 9: Classes—Object-Oriented Programming

Objectives   213
Introduction   213
Summary   241
Lesson 9 Review Questions   241
Testing Your Skills   244

245   Lesson 10: File Input and Output

Objectives   245
Introduction   245
Summary   260
Lesson 10 Review Questions   260
Testing Your Skills   262

263   Index

Try These Projects for More Programming Practice

Exciting new products from South-Western!

Our new C++ and Visual Basic programming activities workbooks offer additional projects that reinforce introductory instruction on these programming languages. These cover everything from beginning, to intermediate, to advanced topics to meet programming needs.

- **NEW! *C++ Programming Projects, Activities Workbook*** (CEP, Inc. & Sestak)
  Has over 10 lessons with 50 projects. Also, there are 30 applications exercises and 11critical thinking projects. These projects number over 35 hours-of -instruction on the most widely used beginning through advanced features of C++.
Text, soft cover, 272 pages	0-538-69081-X
Electronic Instructor CD-ROM Package, 112 pages	0-538-69082-8

Other Complementary Texts:

- ***Introduction to Computer Science Using C++*** (Knowlton)
  Covers computer science fundamentals using the C++ language , and is appropriate for a variety of C++ courses with over 35+ hours-of-instruction.
Text, hard cover, 480 pages	0-538-67600-0
Text/Data Disk Package	0-538-67601-9
Workbook, 288 pages	0-538-67841-0
Instructor's Manual/Solutions Disk Package, 176 pages	0-538-67605-1
NEW! Electronic Instructor CD-ROM	0-538-68799-1
Testing Software	0-538-67604-3

- ***Fundamentals of C++, Understanding Programming and Problem Solving*** (Lambert & Nance)
  is designed for the first course in computer science with over 75+ hours-of-instruction. The text provides a full introduction to the essential features of C++ and emphasizes programming techniques that allow users to solve interesting problems. Programming problems and activities at the end of the chapters allow users to practice the material introduced in the chapter.
Text, hard cover, 808 pages	0-314-20493-8
Lab Manual/Data Disk Package, 200 pages	0-314-22576-5
NEW! Manual/Electronic Instructor CD-ROM Package, 728 pages	0-528-69124-7
Testing Software	0-314-14126-X

- ***ALSO NEW! Visual Basic Programming Projects, Activities Workbook*** (CEP, Inc. & Sestak)
  Has over 10 lessons with 50 projects. Also, there are 30 applications exercises and 11critical thinking projects. These projects number over 35 hours-of -instruction on the most widely used beginning through advanced features of Visual Basic.
Text, soft cover, 272 pages	0-538-68894-7
Electronic Instructor CD-ROM Package, 112 pages	0-538-68895-5

A new feature available for these products is the Electronic Instructor, which includes a printed Instructor's manual and a CD-ROM. The CD-ROM contains tests, lesson plans, all solutions files, and more! Also, ask about our ProgramPaks for compiler software bundles!

Join Us On the Internet
www.swep.com

South-Western
Educational Publishing

List of Projects

Project/Application #	Name	Page #	Project/Application #	Name	Page #
Proj 1-1	Distance Conversions	2	Proj. 6-1C	Two More Functions	147
Proj. 1-2	Checkbook Balancing	7	Proj. 6-1D	Loop For Additional	
App. 1-1		11		Employees	152
App. 1-2		11	App. 6-1		160
App. 1-3		11	App. 6-2		160
Lesson 1	Critical Thinking	12	App. 6-3		160
Proj. 2-1A	Menu Choices	14	Lesson 6	Critical Thinking	161
Proj. 2-1B	Menu Aesthetics	20	Proj. 7-1	Simple Array	164
Proj. 2-1C	Menu Choice Limitations	23	Proj. 7-2	Formatting Array Output	167
Proj. 2-2	Data Input	24	Proj. 7-3	Pointers	169
App. 2-1		32	Proj. 7-4	Initializing An Array From	
App. 2-2		32		User Input	172
App. 2-3		32	Proj. 7-5	Using A Constant Variable To	
Lesson 2	Critical Thinking	34		Set Array Size	174
Proj. 3-1	Decimal to Hexadecimal		Proj. 7-6	Compiling Survey Results	
	and Octal Conversion	36		Using Two Arrays	176
Proj. 3-2	Foreign Currency Conversions	38	Proj. 7-7	Bubble Sort	179
Proj. 3-3	Dollar To Foreign Currency		Proj. 7-8	Searching	182
	Conversions	41	App. 7-1		189
Proj. 3-4	Height Conversion—Feet &		App. 7-2		189
	Inches to Centimeters &		App. 7-3		189
	Meters	44	Lesson 7	Critical Thinking	189
Proj. 3-5	Short Term Loan/Simple		Proj. 8-1	Single Subscript Array	192
	Interest	47	Proj. 8-2	Double Subscript Array	195
Proj. 3-6	Functions	50	Proj. 8-3	Structures	198
Proj. 3-7	Simple Functions	52	Proj. 8-4	Self Referential Structure	202
Proj. 3-8	Header Files	56	Proj. 8-5	Classes	205
App. 3-1		62	App. 8-1		212
App. 3-2		62	App. 8-2		212
App. 3-3		62	App. 8-3		212
Lesson 3	Critical Thinking	63	Lesson 8	Critical Thinking	212
Proj. 4-1	Simple Menu Review	66	Proj. 9-1	A Simple Class	214
Proj. 4-2	Switch Selection Structure	71	Proj. 9-2	An Enhanced Dog—	
Proj. 4-3	Branching Off Of Your Menu	75		Constructors & Destructors	221
Proj. 4-4	If/Else With Existing Programs	83	Proj. 9-3	Inheritance—Derived Classes	225
Proj. 4-5	Using Multiple Selection		Proj. 9-4	Virtual Functions	230
	Structures	86	Proj. 9-5	Multiple Instances Of A Class	235
App. 4-1A		95	App. 9-1		244
App. 4-1B		95	App. 9-2		244
App. 4-1C		95	Lesson 9	Critical Thinking	244
App. 4-1D		95	Proj. 10-1	Create A Sequential Access	
Lesson 4	Critical Thinking	98		File	246
Proj. 5-1	Simple Repetition Overview	100	Proj. 10-2	Reading From A Sequential	
Proj. 5-2	Simple Menu With A While			Access File	249
	Repetition Structure	105	Proj. 10-3	Create An Empty Random	
Proj. 5-3	Repeating A Screen	108		Access File	252
Proj. 5-4	Compound Interest	115	Proj. 10-4	Input Data To A Rando	
Proj. 5-5	Testing For EOF	119		Access File	254
App. 5-1A		127	Proj. 10-5	Reading From A Random	
App. 5-1B		127		Access File	257
App. 5-2		127	App. 10-1		212
Lesson 5	Critical Thinking	128	App. 10-2		262
Proj. 6-1A	The Payroll Program	130	App. 10-3		262
Proj. 6-1B	The Hours Entry Function	139	Lesson 10	Critical Thinking	262

SIMPLE PROGRAMS

Upon completion of this lesson, you should be able to:

■ Describe the parts of a C++ program.

■ Explain the process of program development.

■ Demonstrate your understanding of C++.

■ Produce working applications from the instructions provided.

■ Practice the concepts learned in your programming course.

🕐 **Estimated Time: 1 hour**

Introduction

The purpose of the projects in this lesson is to provide you with a review of simple programs. These projects will allow you to experience immediate success with the knowledge you have gained in your programming course. They are not meant to be difficult; they are simply an opportunity to apply your knowledge to programs that will prove to be useful in the development of your C++ skills and knowledge.

The other, equally important, purpose of these projects is to allow you to have FUN! Programming should not always be serious business. That will happen when someone is giving you a paycheck. Programming should be something that is enjoyed and anticipated! Ask yourself, "Why would I want to continue to do something boring when I can certainly spend the same amount of time on something at which I can have fun?" If you keep this in mind when choosing a possible career path, then computer programming will remain one of your choices.

This lesson presents a few simple programs that will focus on the following:

- **Reviewing the parts of a C++ program.** Even though you have seen these again and again, identifying and understanding the parts of program code needs to become second nature. This will be reinforced through the development, coding, review, and debugging of these programs.

- **Explaining the process of program development.** The process itself, even though simple, reinforces good work habits. Write your code, compile/build the program you have written, allow the compiler to link your code, and run it. Through this repetitive process, you learn to dedicate more time to planning so you spend less time recompiling, linking, and running.

- **Demonstrating your understanding of C++.** Anyone can talk a good game, but if you have working programs to show people, especially potential employers, that carries a great deal more weight than simply using buzzwords. You will develop a better understanding of C++ by reinforcing the practical with a healthy dose of theory through short answer questions and explanations. And you will have opportunities to do this right in this book, next to the exercises on which you are working. This book will become a valuable resource for you.

- **Producing working applications from the instructions provided and practicing the concepts learned in your programming course.** Each lesson is aimed at making you productive. As previously mentioned, this gives you a working demonstration of your abilities. It also gives you a chance to expand on the lessons learned in your programming class. Combined, these lessons will allow you to expand your abilities.

- **Preparing you to design programs that combine all of the concepts used in this book.** An integrated database project that combines the features and applications that you program in each lesson is included on the *Electronic Instructor CD* that accompanies this book. Database management, data warehousing, on-line transaction processing, and electronic commerce are just some of the hot topics in information technology, and they are all built around databases and programming. Throughout these lessons you will be exposed to the fundamentals of this segment of information technology.

So, settle in, get ready to work, and prepare to have fun!

PROJECT 1 - 1 : Distance Conversions (B)

This program will perform the conversion of U.S. distance measurements to metric measurements. This conversion program could be useful to distance runners in converting their runs from miles to kilometers.

Step 1: Start Your Compiler

The projects in this book have been developed using the Microsoft Visual C++ 6.0 compiler. The figures show screens from that program. However, the programs you will be writing will work whether you are using Visual C++ 6.0, an earlier version of it, or a simple text editor.

Figure 1-1 shows the Visual C++ opening screen. The "pane" to the right is the Editor area. It is in this area in which you will be writing the code. It acts just like a text editor.

FIGURE 1-1
Visual C++ opening screen

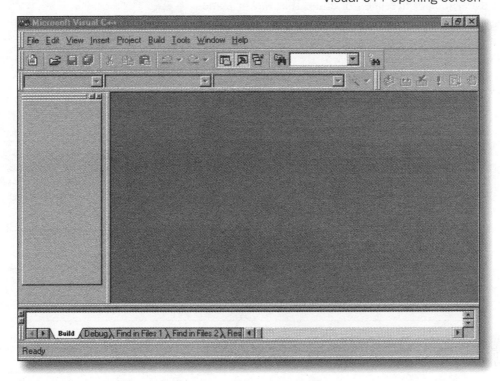

Now that you have your compiler started, begin typing in your code.

Step 2: Type in Your Code

Your code should be typed in as follows:

```cpp
#include <iostream.h>
main()
{
    double MI, KM;

    cout << "Enter the number of miles you've run:  ";
    cin >> MI;

    KM = MI / .62;

    cout <<  MI  <<  " miles is equal to ";
    cout <<  KM  <<  " kilometers." <<  '\n';

    return 0;

}
```

Step 3: Save Your Program

Since this is a short, simple program it wouldn't hurt too much if something happened before you saved your program and you needed to retype it. However, in practice it makes good sense to save your programs early and often. Ideally, you should save after every four or five lines of code. This way, if something should happen, you would not need to retype a great deal of code. Plus it gives you a chance to pause and review your code.

Save your program to disk, naming it **Project 1-1**, or something similar depending on your operating system. Also, place the **.cpp** extension on your file to identify it as a C++ program.

Step 4: Review Your Code

To test your understanding of program components, answer the following questions in the space provided.

1. Explain the #include <iostream.h> line.

   _____

2. Explain main().

   _____

3. What are the { } used for?

   _____

4. What are MI and KM? What is the significance of double?

   _____

5. Explain the cout and the cin commands.

   _____

   _____

6. Explain the line: cout << KM << " kilometers." << '\n';

   _____

   _____

7. Explain the line: cin >> MI;

   _____

8. Explain the line: KM = MI / .62;

   _____

   _____

9. What is the significance of the semicolons?

   _____

HOT TIP

The **.cpp** extension on your program file identifies it as a C++ program. C programs are identified with a **.c** extension.

HOT TIP

In practice you should always save your programs with meaningful file-names. A file named **MI to KM** means more to someone using your program than a name such as **Program1**.

10. What does the / signify in the line KM = MI / .62;?.

_____

11. What is the purpose of `return 0;`?

_____

_____

Reviewing the correct answers to the above questions with your teacher and class will provide you with an overview of the basic components of a C++ program. It's important to know exactly what is happening in your program so that you are able to correct any errors that occur.

Step 5: Build, Link, Run

Enter the commands necessary to build, link, and run your program. If you are running Visual C++ 6.0, simply click on the Build icon. If the Build does not return any errors, then click on the Link icon. If your program links properly, then run it. If errors occur during any of these processes, check your code, correct any errors, and rerun the program.

If you are not using Visual C++ 6.0 as your compiler, then you need to check with your instructor as to the appropriate commands to use to build, link, and run under your compiler. List the name of your compiler and the appropriate commands below:

1. Your compiler: _____

2. Build command: _____

3. Link command: _____

4. Run command: _____

Remember to save your program any time you make changes!

Step 6: Add Comments to Your Code

> **HOT TIP**
>
> The terms *build* and *compile* are used interchangeably.

The biggest complaint you will hear from any programmer, especially those doing maintenance or modification programming, is the lack of documentation included in programs. You should make it a habit to add comments to your code so that you, and those who use it, will have some idea about what's going on in the program.

When should you add comments? You can insert comments either before you begin working on a section, or after the fact. It's easiest to add comments as you are writing the program. This way you have a better idea of what each section is supposed to do, and it assists in the organization of the program. It will also help you remember what it is that you coded.

Add the following comments, shown in bold, to your program code:

```
// Program Name: Project 1-1
// Program Purpose: Miles To Kilometer Conversion
// Programmer: 'Your Name'
#include <iostream.h>

main()
{
    // Declare your variables
    double MI, KM;

    // Get input from the user
    cout << "Enter the number of miles you've run:      ";
    cin >> MI;

    // Convert miles to kilometers
    KM = MI / .62;

    // Output the result to the user
    cout <<  MI  <<  " miles is equal to ";
    cout <<  KM  <<  " kilometers."  <<  '\n';

    // End the main function
    return 0;
}
```

Answer the following questions regarding the comments added to your code:

1. Explain why the comments were added.

_____

_____

2. Explain why the comments were added in these specific places in the code.

_____

_____

3. Would you have added comments in any other area? Why?

_____

_____

4. Would you have modified the comments in any way? Why?

_____

_____

5. In your opinion, are the comments self-explanatory? Explain.

_____

_____

Step 7: Rebuild, Link, and Run Your Program

Changes you make to a program, such as adding comments, can cause the program to not run properly. Any time you make changes to your program, you need to recompile it.

Enter the commands necessary to build, link, and run your program. If you are running Visual C++ 6.0, simply click on the Build icon. If the build does not return any errors, then click on the Link icon. If your program links properly, then run it. If errors occur during any of these processes, check your code, correct any errors, and rerun the program. Remember, it is entirely possible that even a simple program like this can show errors if it is not typed in properly.

If you need to review the commands necessary to build, link, and run under your compiler, see Step 5 above.

Congratulations! You have successfully completed your first simple program. The output should be similar to the following:

```
Enter the number of miles run:  12
12 miles is equal to 19.3548 kilometers
Press any key to continue
```

P R O J E C T   1 - 2 : Checkbook Balancing ⓑ

The next program you write will perform the calculation done on a monthly checking account statement. This calculation takes the balance that the bank says is in your account, adds in any deposits not recorded by the bank, subtracts out checks not recorded by the bank, and provides you with an adjusted bank balance that should be equal to the amount in your checkbook. Obviously, this calculation can easily be performed on a calculator; however, it is good practice for you to request information to be input to the program from a user.

Most of the easy programs you have written and run in your programming classes have probably dealt with YOU providing the necessary values to make the program run by coding the data into your program. This is not the way it works when you really begin to write programs. You create an interface that requests information from the user, and then your program works magic with the user's data!

Even though this calculation is simple, let's use it as a further review of your basic C++ capabilities.

Step 1: Start Your Compiler

If your compiler is not already running, start it now.

Step 2: Type in Your Code

This time, type in the comments as you are typing in the code. As you can see by reviewing the code that follows, there are no comments. It's your job to insert the appropriate comments where necessary. REMEMBER: While you are typing the code, SAVE your program regularly with the name, **Project 1-2**. And make sure you include the **.cpp** extension.

```
#include <iostream.h>

float BankBal, Deposits, SubTotal, Checks, AdjBalance;

main()
{
   cout << "Please enter the balance from your bank statement: ";
   cin >>  BankBal;

   cout << "Please enter the amount of your outstanding deposits: ";
   cin >>  Deposits;

   cout << "Your subtotal is:  ";
   SubTotal = BankBal + Deposits;
   cout << SubTotal << '\n';

   cout << "Please enter the amount of your outstanding checks:  ";
   cin >>  Checks;

   cout << "Your adjusted bank balance is:  ";
   AdjBalance = SubTotal - Checks;
   cout <<  AdjBalance  <<  '\n';

   return 0;
}
```

Answer the following questions regarding the comments added to your code:

1. Explain what comments you added to your code.

_____

_____

2. Explain where your comments were added. Why?

_____

_____

3. Are there any areas in which you did not add comments? Why?

_____

_____

4. In reviewing your comments, would you have modified them in any way? Why?

_____

_____

5. In your opinion, are your comments self-explanatory? Explain.

_____

_____

Step 3: Save Your Program

When you have completed typing the code, save your program once more before moving on to the next step. This way, if anything happens, you will not be forced to retype the code.

Step 4: Build, Link, Run

Enter the commands necessary to build, link, and run your program. If you are running Visual C++ 6.0, simply click on the Build icon. If the build does not return any errors, then click on the Link icon. If your program links properly, then run it. If errors occur during these processes, check your code, correct any errors, and rerun the program.

Remember to save your program any time you make changes!

If you have typed the code correctly, you should now have a second operating program! Congratulations!

Summary

If you compare the first program to the second, you will see that it included a total of seven steps vs. only four in the second project. The four steps presented in the second problem actually represent the four steps of program development: write, compile/build, link, and execute.

Programming is really not that easy. Programming involves problem-solving skills that need to be utilized when your programs do not run or do not run correctly. Understanding the program development cycle is only part of the solution. The major part of the solution is understanding the language in which you are programming.

Beginning with the next lesson, you will be required to provide more input into each project. Remember, the projects presented for you to complete will develop and enhance your C++ skills and knowledge. The fun is only beginning!

LESSON 1 REVIEW QUESTIONS

SHORT ANSWER

Define the following in the space provided.

1. Compiler

2. Text editor

3. Program development

_____

4. .cpp extension

_____

5. Comments

_____

_____

6. Compile

_____

7. Build

_____

8. Link

_____

_____

9. Run

_____

10. Execute

_____

WRITTEN QUESTIONS

Write your answers to the following questions in the space provided.

1. Why should you save your work early and often?

_____

_____

2. Explain the significance of including comments in your code.

_____

3. Identify and explain the main sections of a C++ program.

_____

_____

_____

4. Discuss some of the more common errors that you have found when debugging programs you have written.

_____

_____

_____

TESTING YOUR SKILLS

SCANS

Estimated Time:
Application 1-1 30 minutes
Application 1-2 30 minutes
Application 1-3 30 minutes

APPLICATION 1-1 B

1. Add code to Project 1-1 that converts kilometers into miles.
   a. Open the **Project 1-1** program file.
   b. After the code that creates the output of the miles to kilometers conversion, add the necessary lines to perform a kilometers to miles conversion. The lines of code should be similar to the code used for the original program.

   HINT: The conversion this time is going in reverse. Use your algebra skills!

   c. Save your revised program as **App1-1**.

APPLICATION 1-2 B

1. Explain each line of code in Project 1-2.
   a. Open **Project 1-2**.
   b. On each line below, write a short explanation for the corresponding line of code. Remember that the lines of code in a C++ program are not numbered. You will need to count each line beginning with the very first line of the program.

   HINT: Comment lines and blank lines also count as a line of code.

1. _____

2. _____

3. _____

4. _____

5. _____

6. _____

7. _____

8. _____

9. _____

10. _____

11. _____

1 1

12. _____

13. _____

14. _____

15. _____

16. _____

17. _____

18. _____

19. _____

20. _____

21. _____

22. _____

23. _____

24. _____

25. _____

APPLICATION 1-3

1. Modify Project 1-2 so that the dollar amounts are aligned.
    a. Open the **Project 1-2** file.
    b. Add spaces to each output line so that the dollar amounts are aligned.

    HINT: You may need to build, link, and run this a few times until you get it right.

    c. Save this revised project as **App1-3**.

CRITICAL THINKING

 Estimated Time: 1 hour

SCANS

Write a program, similar to Project 1-1, that converts Fahrenheit temperature to Celsius and back again.

USER INTERACTION

OBJECTIVES

Upon completion of this lesson, you should be able to:

- Define user interaction.
- Explain the reasons for user interaction.
- Design interfaces for user interaction.
- Integrate checks into user interfaces.
- Produce working applications from the instructions provided.

 Estimated Time: 4 hours

Introduction

In programming, ***user interaction*** simply means that the user is enabled to control certain aspects of a program. Every computer program is written for someone. Who that someone is and what they need the program to do for them is a very important part of program design. You, as the programmer, need to identify these ***end users*** and gather information from them. The information you gather not only provides you with valuable information about the coding of the program, but it also gives you an idea of how the program should be presented in order to make it ***user-friendly***.

In general, programs do only a few things: They gather information from the user; they process information; they output information; and they store information. The specifics of each of these functions depend on the needs of the user. Although there are some functions that the program performs "behind the scenes," without the involvement of the user, most programs require the user to exercise some control over its operations. That is, the user must interact with the program in order to get from it what he or she needs. The starting point for this interaction, as well as providing control limitations, is the ***user interface***.

The user interface can be as simple as a text menu, or it can be an elaborate design of menu bars, text boxes, command buttons, and other graphical user interface (GUI) objects found in most of the software used today. Regardless, the function is the same: to gather information from the user so that the program can perform the operations required by the user. The user interface is also the mechanism through which control of programming operations is determined. If there is *not* a menu option for a specific procedure, then the user cannot choose to perform that procedure. This leaves control in the "hands" of the program. As you can see, user interaction is a very important part of programming.

This lesson will focus on the following:

- **User interaction.** The topics discussed in this introduction will be reinforced throughout the lesson. User interaction is a very important part of programming and needs to become second nature.

- **The reasons for user interaction.** As you code your programs, each step will be explained thoroughly so that you will understand the significance. In addition, the user-friendly concept of a program will be continually addressed. You hear a lot of talk about the "user-friendliness" of a program. If you design an *intuitive* interface, this will only increase the friendliness of your program.

- **Designing interfaces for user interaction.** Each of the projects in this lesson will result in a completed interface. You will concentrate on user input and program output. You will also touch on *aesthetics*—a term used when talking about the attractiveness and common sense of the interface design.

- **Integrating checks into your user interfaces.** There will be times when users will need to verify the actions they have performed or have chosen to perform. For example, when deciding to delete a file, users are usually prompted with a *confirm* question. This question is usually, "Are you sure you want to do this?" You will learn about checks that should be built into interfaces.

- **Producing working applications from the instructions provided.** You will code working applications in every lesson in this book. There is no better way to learn how to program than to program!

So, strap yourself in, get ready to work, and prepare to have fun!

PROJECT 2-1A : Menu Choices Ⓑ

In Lesson 1, your projects used very simple interfaces. For example, in Project 1-1 you simply asked the user to input the number of miles run, and in Project 1-2 you asked the user to input three predetermined values.

Now you will create an interface that provides users with a method through which they can input data into the program. You will begin with a simple interface and modify it to include the controls mentioned in the Introduction.

Step 1: Start Your Compiler

The projects in this book have been developed using the Microsoft Visual C++ 6.0 compiler. However, the programs you will be writing will work whether you are using a simple text editor, Visual C++ 6.0, or an earlier version of it.

Now that you've started your compiler, you can begin typing in code.

Step 2: Type in Your Code

Type your code exactly as shown below. Remember to save your work as you type. Save this program with the name **Project 2-1A.cpp**.

```
// Project 2-1A
// Programmer: (Your Name)
// This program will introduce the basics of creating a simple menu.

#include <iostream.h>

// The main function

main()
{

// Initialize the menu choice variable

int Choice;


// The following displays the user's menu choices on the screen

   cout << "1) Add A New Record";
   cout << "2) Modify An Existing Record";
   cout << "3) Delete An Existing Record";
   cout << "4) View/Print An Existing Record";
   cout << "5) Exit \n";
   cout << "Please Enter Your Choice:  ";

// The cin command accepts the user's choice

   cin >> Choice;

// The following IF statements provide output based on the user's choice.

   if (Choice == 1)
       cout << "You chose to add a new record.";

   if (Choice == 2)
       cout << "You chose to modify a record.";

   if (Choice == 3)
       cout << "You chose to delete a record.";

   if (Choice == 4)
       cout << "You chose to view/print a record.";

   if (Choice == 5)
       cout << "You chose to Exit this menu.";

// The return statement ends the function.

   return 0;

}
```

Step 3: Review Your Code

To test your understanding of the program components, answer the following questions in the space provided.

1. Explain the `#include <iostream.h>` line.

_____

_____

2. Explain `main()`.

_____

3. What are the { } used for?

_____

4. What is `Choice`? What is the significance of `int`?

_____

_____

5. Explain the `cout` and the `cin` commands.

_____

6. What is the significance of the semicolons?

_____

7. Explain the `if` command.

_____

8. Explain the following line of code: `if (Choice == 1)`.

_____

9. Explain the sequence of the five `if` statements.

_____

_____

_____

10. What is the purpose of: `return 0;`?

_____

11. Explain the use of white space.

_____

Reviewing the correct answers to the above questions with your teacher and class will provide you with an overview of the basic components of a C++ program. It's important to know exactly what is happening in your program so that you are able to correct any errors that occur.

Step 4: Build, Link, Run

Enter the commands necessary to build, link, and run your program. If you are running Visual C++ 6.0, simply click on the Build icon. If the build does not return any errors, then click on the Link icon. If your program links properly, then run it. If errors occur during any of these processes, check your code, correct any errors, and rerun the program.

If you are not using Visual C++ 6.0 as your compiler, then you need to review the commands you used in Lesson 1. Fill in the name of your compiler and the appropriate commands below.

Your Compiler: _____

Build command: _____

Link command: _____

Run command: _____

Remember to save your program any time you make changes!

Step 5: Review Your Output

Your output should look like the following:

```
1) Add A New Record2) Modify An Existing Record3) Delete An Existing Record 4)Vi
Ew/Print An Existing Record5) Exit
Please Enter Your Choice:  __
```

Answer the following questions regarding the output:

1. Why is the output jumbled together?

_____

2. What can be done to separate and organize the output?

_____

3. What type of character is \n?

_____

4. What is the purpose of \n?

_____

5. Why should we organize the output to the screen?

_____

_____

Using Escape Characters

The output is jumbled because even though you have placed the code on separate lines within the program, that does *not* translate into separate lines on the screen. You have told the program to display five separate statements on the screen; you did *not* tell the program to display those statements on five separate lines. In order to separate and organize the output you need to use escape characters.

Escape characters are characters that follow a back-slash. The **backslash** itself is known as the escape character. The characters following the backslash are simply known as characters. However, to make life simpler, think of the entire combination as the escape character.

Escape characters signal the program to format the line to be output, or to insert a character into the line. For example, the \n means *new line*. This signals the program to output whatever follows on a new line. Table 2-1 lists additional escape characters and their meanings.

Step 6: Modify the Output

By using escape characters, you can arrange the output to the screen. Try arranging your output by adding the following escape characters, shown in bold and underlined, to your code.

TABLE 2-1
Escape characters

CHARACTER	MEANING
\t	Tab
\b	Backspace
\"	Double quote
\'	Single quote
\?	Question mark
\\	Backslash

```
// Project 2-1A
// Programmer: (Your Name)
// This program will introduce the basics of creating
// a simple menu.

#include <iostream.h>


// The main function

main()
{

// Initialize the menu choice variable

int Choice;


// The following displays your menu choices on the screen

   cout << "1) Add A New Record \n";
   cout << "2) Modify An Existing Record \n";
   cout << "3) Delete An Existing Record \n";
   cout << "4) View/Print An Existing Record \n";
   cout << "5) Exit \n";
   cout << "\nPlease Enter Your Choice:   ";

// The cin command accepts the user's choice

   cin >> Choice;

// The following IF statements provide output based on your choice.
```

```
    if (Choice == 1)
        cout << "\nYou chose to add a new record. \n";

    if (Choice == 2)
        cout << "\nYou chose to modify a record. \n";

    if (Choice == 3)
        cout << "\nYou chose to delete a record. \n";

    if (Choice == 4)
        cout << "\nYou chose to view/print a record. \n";

    if (Choice == 5)
        cout << "\nYou chose to Exit this menu. \n";

// The return statement ends the function.

    return 0;

}
```

Before moving on to the next step, write a description in the space below of what you think the escape characters will do to your output, or simply write out the new output as it should appear on screen.

_____

_____

_____

_____

_____

_____

_____

Step 7: Rebuild, Link, and Run Your Program

As mentioned before, changes you make to a program, such as adding comments, can cause the program to not run properly. Any time you make changes to your program, you need to recompile it.

Enter the commands necessary to build, link, and run your program. If you are running Visual C++ 6.0, simply click on the Build icon. If the build does not return any errors, then click on the Link icon. If your program links properly, then run it. If errors occur during any of these processes, check your code, correct any errors, and rerun the program. Remember, it is entirely possible that even a simple program like this can show errors if it is not typed in properly.

If you need to review the commands necessary to build, link, and run under your compiler, then see Step 4 above. Make sure you are continuously saving your program.

Step 8: Review Your Output

Your output should look similar to the following:

```
1)  Add A New Record
2)  Modify An Existing Record
```

```
3)  Delete An Existing Record
4)  View/Print An Existing Record
5)  Exit

Please Enter Your Choice:  __
The response to your choice will be displayed here.
Press any key to continue
```

Now that your output looks organized, answer the following in the space provided.

1. What does the \n escape character do when placed at the end of a line?

_____

2. What does the \n escape character do when placed before the output?

_____

3. What does the \n escape character do when placed at both the beginning and the end of an output line?

_____

_____

If you are not sure of the answers to the above questions—experiment! Remove one of the escape characters and see what the output looks like. Try removing one of the escape characters from the front of a line on which you've placed two escape characters. Then go back and answer the review questions.

P R O J E C T   2 - 1 B : Menu Aesthetics

This program will build on the program you completed in Project 2-1A. Now that you have your menu, and it looks good, you will enhance it!

What is this menu to be used for? For what program, and for what purpose? From reading the menu you know it deals with file manipulations, but you need to know more. The simple menu, at this point, can be used for *any* program since all programs usually incorporate these commands. That's one of the reasons you'll be keeping this file, so you can reuse it with other programs. But you need to make this menu more specific so that it is appropriate for the program you are writing.

Step 1: Start Your Compiler

If your compiler is not already running, start it now.

Step 2: Type in Your Code

Type in the code as shown below. Save the program as **Project 2-1B**. Make sure you include the **.cpp** extension. *Remember:* Save your program regularly as you type the code.

 HOT TIP

More experienced programmers may want to make a copy of the *Project 2-1A.cpp* file, rename it **Project 2-1B.cpp**, and then insert the new code where appropriate. Make sure your final code matches what's shown.

```
// Project 2-1B
// Programmer: (Your Name)
// This program will introduce the basics of creating
// a heading and adding an aesthetic touch to a simple menu.

#include <iostream.h>

// The main function

main()
{

// Initialize the menu choice variable

int Choice;


// The following creates a heading for our menu.

    cout  << "\t\t\t/////////////////////////////\n";
    cout  << "\t\t\t/////////   RECORD   /////////\n";
    cout  << "\t\t\t/////////    MENU    /////////\n";
    cout  << "\t\t\t/////////////////////////////\n";

// The following displays your menu choices on the screen

    cout << "\n\t\t\t1) Add A New Record \n";
    cout << "\t\t\t2) Modify An Existing Record \n";
    cout << "\t\t\t3) Delete An Existing Record \n";
    cout << "\t\t\t4) View/Print An Existing Record \n";
    cout << "\t\t\t5) Exit \n";
    cout << "\n\t\t\tPlease Enter Your Choice:  ";

// The cin command accepts the user's choice

    cin >> Choice;

// The following IF statements provide output based on your choice.

    if (Choice == 1)
        cout << "\n\t\t\tYou chose to add a new record.\n\t\t\t";

    if (Choice == 2)
        cout << "\n\t\t\tYou chose to modify a record.\n\t\t\t";

    if (Choice == 3)
        cout << "\n\t\t\tYou chose to delete a record.\n\t\t\t";

    if (Choice == 4)
        cout << "\n\t\t\tYou chose to view/print a record.\n\t\t\t";

    if (Choice == 5)
        cout << "\n\t\t\tYou chose to Exit this menu.\n\t\t\t";
```

```
// The return statement ends the function.

   return 0;

}
```

Answer the following questions regarding the above code:

1. Explain what each of the `cout` commands do in the heading area.

_____

_____

_____

_____

2. Explain, in general, what the \n and the \t escape characters do.

_____

_____

3. Explain the following line of code:

```
cout << "\n\t\t\t1) Add A New Record \n";
```

_____

_____

4. Explain the following line of code:

```
if (Choice == 1)
    cout << "\n\t\t\tYou chose to add a new record.\n\t\t\t";
```

_____

_____

_____

5. Explain the following line of code:

```
cout << "\n\t\t\tPlease Enter Your Choice:   ";
```

_____

_____

Step 3: Save Your Program

When you have completed typing the code, save your program once more before moving on to the next step.

Step 4: Build, Link, Run

Enter the commands necessary to build, link, and run your program. If errors occur during any of these processes, check your code, correct any errors, and rerun the program.

Remember to save your program any time you make changes!

If you have typed the code correctly, you should now have an enhanced menu that looks something like the following:

```
//////////////////////////
////////  Record  //////////
//////////  Menu   //////////
//////////////////////////
1)    Add A New Record
2)    Modify An Existing Record
3)    Delete An Existing Record
4)    View/Print An Existing Record
5)    Exit

Please Enter Your Choice:  __
Your response displays here.
Press any key to continue
```

Congratulations! You now have an enhanced menu that looks neat and organized!

P R O J E C T   2 - 1 C : Menu Choice Limitations

There is one last item to take care of in regard to menus. If you haven't tried it, rerun the *Project 2-1B* program and input a choice *not* listed on the menu. Guess what? It doesn't display a message but still runs! It doesn't do what it should do—it simply "hangs," or does nothing. This should *not* happen with a menu! Click the exit button on the program window to end the program.

Menus are meant to provide users with options, and to provide the program with control. Any commands or operations that are *not* listed on a menu should *not* be executable by the user.

The third part of this project will limit the user's choices to those listed on the menu.

Step 1: Start Your Compiler

If your compiler is not already running, start it now.

Step 2: Type in Your Code

Open **Project 2-1B** and save the file with the name **Project 2-1C.cpp**. Add the new code shown below in bold and underlined to the program.

```
if (Choice == 4)
    cout << "\n\t\t\tYou chose to view/print a record.\n\t\t\t";

if (Choice == 5)
    cout << "\n\t\t\tYou chose to Exit this menu.\n\t\t\t";

if ((Choice != 1) && (Choice != 2) && (Choice != 3) && (Choice !=  4) &&
    (Choice != 5))
```

```
         cout << "\n\t\t\tYour choice is NOT valid! Please enter a
         CORRECT choice!\n\t\t\t";

// The return statement ends the function.

   return 0;

}
```

Step 3: Save Your Program

When you have completed typing the code, save your program once more before moving on to the next step.

Step 4: Build, Link, Run

Enter the commands necessary to build, link, and run your program. If errors occur during any of these processes, check your code, correct any errors, and rerun the program.

Remember to save your program any time you make changes!

If you have typed the code correctly, you should now receive an error message when you type in anything except 1, 2, 3, 4, or 5. However, you will also notice that the menu simply ends regardless of which choice you make, whether it's correct or incorrect. This is not the way the menu will behave when finished; however, the topics needed to make the menu operate properly will be forthcoming in Lessons 4, 5, and 6.

P R O J E C T   2 - 2 : Data Input (B)

Users will also require interfaces through which they enter data in the program. Menus are one simple way of enabling the user to make choices, but as you know, a program often needs more information from the user, and making a simple menu choice just won't suffice. For example, a database program may require the user to provide names, addresses, telephone numbers, E-mail addresses, Web sites, and maybe even pictures and sound files. The database programmer must create a way for the user to input such information in the program. This project focuses on the design and coding of a data input interface.

Step 1: Start Your Compiler

If your compiler is not already running, start it now.

Step 2: Type in Your Code

Type in the code as shown below. Save the program as **Project 2-2.cpp**. *Remember:* Save often as you type in the code.

```
// Project 2-2
// Programmer: <Your Name Here>
// This program will show the design of a data input screen.

// Include the header file necessary for input and output.
```

```cpp
#include <iostream.h>

// The main function begins.

main()
{
    // Initialize the necessary variables.

    char fname[20];      // First Name
    char mi[1];    // Middle Initial
    char lname[30];      // Last Name
    char phnum[7];         // Phone Number not including area code
    char dob[10]; // Date of Birth, Format MM/DD/YYYY
    char email[30];      // E-mail address

    // Set up the input screen
    // Create the Heading

    cout << "\t\t\t%%%%%%%%%%%%%%%%%%%%%%%%%%%%%\n";
    cout << "\t\t\t%%%%%% Contact Name %%%%%%\n";
    cout << "\t\t\t%%%%%%%%%%%% and %%%%%%%%%%%%\n";
    cout << "\t\t\t%%%%%%%%%% Address %%%%%%%%%%\n";
    cout << "\t\t\t%%%%%%%%%%%%%%%%%%%%%%%%%%%%%\n";

    // Inform the user as to what this screen is to be used for.

    cout << "\n\n\tUse this screen to input a new contact to your Personal
        Phone Book.\n";

    // Get the user to enter information.

    cout << "\n\nEnter Contact's First Name:\t";
    cin >> fname;

    cout << "\nEnter Contact's Middle Initial:\t";
    cin >> mi;

    cout << "\nEnter Contact's Last Name:\t";
    cin >> lname;

    cout << "\nEnter Contact's Phone Number\n";
    cout << "(without the area code):\t";
    cin >> phnum;

    cout << "\nEnter Contact's Date of Birth:\n";
    cout << "(use MM/DD/YYYY format):\t";
    cin >> dob;

    cout << "\nEnter Contact's E-Mail Address:\t";
    cin >> email;

    cout << "\n";

    return 0;
}
```

Step 3: Save Your Program

When you have completed typing the code, save your program once more before moving on to the next step.

Step 4: Build, Link, Run

Enter the commands necessary to build, link, and run your program. If errors occur during any of these processes, check your code, correct any errors, and rerun the program.

Remember to save your program any time you make changes!

Your output should look like the following:

```
%%%%%%%%%%%%%%%%%%%%%%%%%%%%
%%%%%  Contact Name  %%%%%
%%%%%%%%    and    %%%%%%%%%
%%%%%%%%  Address   %%%%%%%%
%%%%%%%%%%%%%%%%%%%%%%%%%%%%

Use this screen to input a new contact to your Personal Phone Book.

Enter Contact's First Name:
Enter Contact's Middle Initial:
Enter Contact's Last Name:
Enter Contact's Phone Number
(without the area code):
Enter Contact's Date of Birth
(use MM/DD/YYYY format):
Enter Contact's E-mail Address:
Press any key to continue
```

You need to be aware of a few things regarding this program: Error-checking is *not* being performed; therefore, you can enter anything into any field and it will be accepted. If you press the Enter key without entering a value, the program will not respond to anything *except* the Enter key. Otherwise, the program should work. *Remember,* you are designing an interface, not coding a working menu. The "guts" of the menu will come in Lessons 4, 5, and 6.

Building **objects**, or program components, like these is actually referred to as **object-oriented programming**. We are building components that can be reused in other programs.

Step 5: Explain Your Program

Explain each line or block of code in the program in the space provided below.

```
// Project 2-2
// Programmer: <Your Name Here>
// This program will show the design of a data input screen.
```

_____

_____

```
// Include the header file necessary for input and output.

#include <iostream.h>
```

```
// The main function begins.

main()
{
```

```
// Initialize the necessary variables.

char fname[20];        // First Name
char mi[1];    // Middle Initial
char lname[30];        // Last Name
char phnum[7];         // Phone Number not including area code
char dob[10]; // Date of Birth, Format MM/DD/YYYY
char email[30];        // E-mail address
```

```
// Set up the input screen
// Create the Heading

cout << "\t\t\t%%%%%%%%%%%%%%%%%%%%%%%%%%%%%%%\n";
cout << "\t\t\t%%%%%% Contact Name %%%%%%\n";
cout << "\t\t\t%%%%%%%%%% and %%%%%%%%%%\n";
cout << "\t\t\t%%%%%%%%% Address %%%%%%%%%\n";
cout << "\t\t\t%%%%%%%%%%%%%%%%%%%%%%%%%%%%%%%\n";
```

```
// Inform the user as to what this screen is to be used for.

cout << "\n\n\tUse this screen to input a new contact to your Personal
    Phone Book.\n";
```

```
// Get the user to enter information.

cout << "\n\nEnter Contact's First Name:\t";
cin >> fname;
```

```
cout << "\nEnter Contact's Middle Initial:\t";
cin >> mi;
```

```
cout << "\nEnter Contact's Last Name:\t";
cin >> lname;
```

```
cout << "\nEnter Contact's Phone Number\n";
cout << "(without the area code):\t";
cin >> phnum;
```

```
cout << "\nEnter Contact's Date of Birth:\n";
cout << "(use MM/DD/YYYY format):\t";
cin >> dob;
```

```
cout << "\nEnter Contact's E-Mail Address:\t";
cin >> email;
```

```
cout << "\n";
```

```
    return 0;
}
```

_____

_____

_____

Additional Functions

There are two additional functions that you will eventually add to this menu. The first is an option for users to verify the data that they entered. If the data is correct, which the users will tell the program after checking the data, then the data will be saved. If not, then the data will be removed from the variables and the users can input the data again. The second is an option to terminate the adding of records, or to continue and add more records.

You will add these functions to the program in Lessons 4, 5, and 6. These functions are mentioned here because they are important when considering the design of the user interface. Your menus should have built-in safeguards to make users aware of their actions. Remember this when designing the layout of your other menus and screens.

Summary

This lesson focused on user interaction and how to empower the user to control certain aspects of a program. The first half of this lesson focused on menu design as a mechanism for user interaction with a program. You learned how to organize and enhance a menu by adding a heading, aligning the menu choices, adding some spacing between the lines, and limiting user choices to those listed on the menu.

The aesthetics of an interface—how logical and neat the interface looks—were discussed. This aspect of programming also touches on the user-friendliness of a program. Can the user operate the program without breaking into a sweat? Is it intuitive? Is it logical? Or, is the user continually frustrated at the way the program operates?

You then explored the data input interface. Before a program can do anything, it must have data to process. That's where these types of interfaces come into play. They assist the program in getting data from the user.

You have also touched slightly on objects and object-oriented programming. The components you create throughout this project book can be used over and over again.

SHORT ANSWER

Define the following in the space provided.

1. User interaction

_____

2. End user

_____

3. User-friendly

_____

4. Control

_____

_____

_____

5. GUI

_____

_____

6. Intuitive

_____

_____

7. Aesthetics

_____

8. Confirm

_____

_____

9. Escape characters

_____

_____

10. Backslash

_____

11. Objects

_____

_____

12. Object-oriented programming

_____

13. Error-checking

_____

14. Verify input

_____

_____

15. Terminate the program

_____

16. Modify a record

_____

17. Delete a record

_____

18. View a record

_____

19. Print a record

_____

WRITTEN QUESTIONS

Write your answers to the following questions in the space provided.

1. Why is it important that a program is user-friendly?

_____

_____

2. Explain the purpose of a user interface.

_____

_____

3. Explain how a user interface can provide the user with control over a program.

_____

_____

4. Explain aesthetics in terms of computer programming.

_____

_____

5. List the seven escape characters. Explain what each escape character does.

_____

_____

_____

_____

_____

_____

_____

6. Explain the following line of code. (This statement is pulled from Step 2 of Project 2-1C.)

```
if ((Choice != 1) && (Choice != 2) && (Choice != 3) && (Choice != 4) &&
    (Choice != 5))
cout << "\n\t\t\tYour choice is NOT valid! Please enter a CORRECT
    choice!\n\t\t\t";
```

_____

_____

_____

7. List and explain at least three types of "checks" that you should build into a user interface.

_____

_____

_____

_____

_____

TESTING YOUR SKILLS

 Estimated Time:

Application 2-1 1 hour
Application 2-2 1 hour
Application 2-3 1 hour

When you begin work on the Applications below, make sure you take time to scan through other software packages to see how they handle these menu choices.

APPLICATION 2-1

In Project 2-2 you built a data input interface for adding a new record to a database (a personal phone book). That same interface could be used if Choice #1 from the menu in Project 2-1C is selected. Create an interface for the *MODIFY* menu item in Project 2-1C. When you *modify* a record, you first need to display it to see if it is the correct record and then you need to modify the information that has changed. Use the Project 2-2 code and screen design as a "template" for the new interface.

1. Open the **Project 2-1C.cpp** program file.

2. Print out the code to this program.

3. Run the program so that you can see the screen format.

4. On scratch paper, manually design possible layouts for each additional screen, one at a time. You might want to number each line so you can choose which item to modify.

5. Using Project 2-1C code as an example, code your screen layouts. Do not worry about the function of the menu—only code the layout.

APPLICATION 2-2

Create an interface screen for the *DELETE* menu item in Project 2-1C. When you choose to *delete* a record you first need to make sure you are deleting the correct record. Use the code and screen design for Project 2-2 as a "template" for the interface.

1. Open the **Project 2-1C.cpp** program file.

2. Print out the code to this program.

3. Run the program so that you can see the screen format.

4. On scratch paper, manually design possible layouts for each additional screen, one at a time. (*Hint:* Here we are trying to get rid of a specific record. Including a check line similar to, "Is this the record you want to delete?" is a good idea.)

5. Using Project 2-1C code as an example, code your screen layouts. Do *not* worry about the function of the menu—only code the layout.

APPLICATION 2-3

Create an interface screen for the *VIEW/PRINT* menu item in Project 2-1C. This menu choice will most likely present another menu that provides a list of viewing or printing choices to be selected by the user. Use the code and screen design for Project 2-2 as a "template" for the interface.

1. Open the **Project 2-1C.cpp** program file.

2. Print out the code to this program.

3. Run the program so that you can see the screen format.

4. On scratch paper, manually design possible layouts for each additional screen, one at a time. (*Hint:* This menu item may lead to another more detailed menu. Does the user want to view or print? Can the print option be separate from the view option? Is there only one option, the "combined" VIEW/PRINT? You decide.)

5. Using Project 2-1C code as an example, code your screen layouts. Do *not* worry about the function of the menu—only code the layout.

In this lesson you focused on the creation of two types of user interfaces. One provided the user with choices to make in regard to program action. The second provided the user with an interface through which data could be entered in a record. In the Applications above, you were required to create interfaces from the other menu choices.

However, there are many types of other interfaces that can make your program easier to use, as well as enabling the program to maintain control over its operation. For example, when you log on to your school's network you may be asked for a user name and password, or when you want to open a file you need to select a drive, folder and so on, to create a path to that file.

Your Critical Thinking assignment is to create two additional user interfaces, not included in this lesson, using the two questions below as guidelines:

1. What *kind* of information will I be keeping track of?

2. What do I want to *do* with the information?

Once you have answered these questions, you can begin designing your user interfaces. Good luck and have fun!

CALCULATIONS

OBJECTIVES

Upon completion of this lesson, you should be able to:

■ Explain the purpose of calculations.

■ Explain the advantages and disadvantages of performing calculations vs. storing values.

■ Demonstrate the appropriate use of calculations vs. storing values.

■ Demonstrate the proper use of variables in calculations.

■ Relate your calculations to user interaction.

■ Translate math formula into code.

■ Design code for including calculations in programs.

■ Distinguish precedence among the order of operators.

■ Organize your code into functions.

🕑 **Estimated Time: 6 1/2 hours**

Introduction

Calculations are an important part of any computer program. Computers are always calculating something. It may be interest on a past due invoice; it may be payroll; it may be sports statistics; or it may be subtracting money from your checking account every time you use your ATM. Historically, and even today, computers have been used as "super calculators."

The main purpose of a calculation is to find an answer. The end user needs to know something, so he or she "asks" the computer to perform the calculation. Why? Because the computer does it faster, and if it's programmed right, it won't make a mistake. Just like with user interfaces, calculations help make life easier for the end user.

This lesson will focus on the following:

■ **The purpose of calculations.** The purpose behind including calculations in code will be continuously explained. It's not enough to know how; you also need to know why.

■ **The advantages and disadvantages of performing calculations vs. storing values, and the appropriate use of calculations vs. storing values.** When you develop code for a program, you will notice there are instances where the calculation is performed and the answer is output, but the answer is never stored. There are some calculations that are so simple and quick, that it makes more sense to perform the calculation when the answer is needed than to store the answer again and again in a file. For example, if you know that an employee worked 36 regular hours and 0 overtime hours, then you know the total hours, or you can calculate it very quickly.

■ **The proper use of variables in calculations and how to relate calculations to user interaction.** As mentioned above, you will be performing calculations needed by the end user. Therefore, you will need to gather information from the end user in order to perform the calculation so that it benefits that particular end user. The only way to get input from the end user is to use variables through a user interface, and these variables need to be defined and used properly.

■ **Translating math formulas into code, designing code for including calculations in programs, distinguishing precedence among the order of operators, and analyzing your programs to determine their correctness.** These four objectives basically translate into programming. You will decide what calculations you need to perform, and then you will find the appropriate math formula. At that point, you will begin to translate the formula into code. You will need to pay particular attention to precedence in order to make sure complex formulas are performed correctly. Finally, you will review the answer to make sure the formula calculation performed correctly.

■ **Organizing your code into functions.** A lot of the calculations that your code will be performing are generic. For example, adding sales tax to an invoice, calculating interest, or calculating sports statistics, are basically generic calculations. The calculations are performed the same, only the input varies. If you save these calculations as functions, then you can use them over and over *without* having to retype the code. You simply call the function.

■ **Producing working applications from the instructions provided.** You will code working applications in every lesson in this book. There is no better way to learn how to program than to program.

So, remember your math, get ready to work, and prepare to have fun!

P R O J E C T   3 - 1 :
Decimal to Hexadecimal and Octal Conversion   (B)

Once again you will start with simple programs and work your way into harder projects. In this lesson you will be required to do some research and coding on your own. Nothing too hard, just enough to introduce you to what programmers *really* go through in coding their programs.

This project will perform decimal integer to hexadecimal and octal conversions. *Manipulators* inserted into the *cout* statement will perform the conversion calculation itself. Even though this is a shortcut, don't feel slighted because there are many items built into C++ that will make your programming jobs easier for you. These *objects* can be reused in many different programs, many different times, without needing to code them into each program. You will be doing the same with the calculations you create in these projects.

Step 1: Start Your Compiler

The projects in this book have been developed using the Microsoft Visual C++ 6.0 compiler. However, the programs you will be writing will work whether you are using 6.0, an earlier version of Visual C++, or a simple text editor.

Now that you've started your compiler, you can begin typing in code.

Step 2: Type in Your Code

Your code should be typed in exactly as follows. Remember to save your code after typing in the first line or two of your program, and then as often as possible thereafter. Save this program with the name **Project 3-1.cpp**. As you enter the code, notice the new *header* file added after the iostream header file, and the *hex* and *oct* manipulators included in the final two cout lines.

```cpp
#include <iostream.h>
#include <iomanip.h>

main()
{
    int inNum;


    cout << "Please input a number:  ";
    cin >> inNum;

    cout  << hex << "This is the number in Hex:   " << inNum << "\n";
    cout  << oct << "This is the number in Octal:  " << inNum << "\n";

    return 0;

}
```

Step 3: Save Your Program

Once you have finished typing in your code, save your code one final time before compiling your program.

Step 4: Build, Link, Run

Enter the commands necessary to build, link, and run your program. If you are running Visual C++ 6.0, simply click on the Build icon. If the build does not return any errors, then click on the Link icon. If your program links properly, then run it. If errors occur during any of these processes, check your code, correct any errors, and rerun the program.

If you are not using Visual C++ 6.0 as your compiler, then use the appropriate commands for your compiler. You should now be familiar with those commands.

 HOT TIP

Visual C++ 6.0 users: Instead of clicking the Build icon every time, you can bypass that step and click the Link icon. By clicking the Link icon, the build happens first and will still show any errors. You simply have one less button to click.

Step 5: Review Your Code

Now that your program has run successfully, answer the following questions about the new code introduced in this project. Review the introductory comments preceding this project for additional help.

1. Explain the *preprocessor* command line: `#include <iomanip.h>`. (*Hint*: Filenames are limited to eight characters because many C++ compilers work on operating systems that do not support long filenames. Therefore, many of the filenames are abbreviated versions of what they actually are to be used for. Use this hint to explain the iomanip.h file.)

_____

_____

2. Explain the *hex* manipulator.

_____

3. Explain the *oct* manipulator.

_____

4. Explain why inNum is an integer variable type.

_____

Step 6: Add Comments to Your Code

Add the appropriate comments in the appropriate places in your code. When you are finished, save your program.

1. List your comments, explain where they were placed, and explain why.

_____

_____

_____

Step 7: Rebuild, Link, and Run Your Program

Changes you make to your program, even the simple insertion of comments, can cause your program to not run properly. Any time you modify your code, you need to recompile it. If any errors occur during this step, review the comments you entered and correct any errors.

Congratulations! You now have a very easy program that will convert decimal integers to both hexadecimal and octal numbers.

P R O J E C T 3 - 2 : Foreign Currency Conversions

If you haven't noticed, the world is becoming smaller. With the Internet we have instant access to anyone in the world who's connected. Getting information from one country to another is becoming easier and easier.

In light of this, many businesses, both large and small, are developing a global customer base. One of the concerns in the financial world is the conversion of foreign currency into dollars and vice versa. What makes this conversion especially difficult is that the values of most currencies are not fixed—they float (or fluctuate). Because of this, businesses need to keep track of currency values daily. You are going to code two programs that will help them do just that. The first project will convert foreign currency into dollars; the second will reverse the conversion.

You are also going to be expected to start remembering how to code the appropriate input for your programs. With this project, you will be asked to do more and more of the work. After all, it's what programmers are paid big bucks to do!

Step 1: Code the General Outline of the Main()

If you review all the programs you've coded, you will notice that the Main() has a general layout. Write it down here and then start your compiler.

_____

_____

_____

_____

_____

_____

Step 2: Start Your Compiler

If you need to, review previous projects in order to complete this step.

Step 3: Type in Your Code

Type in your code exactly as shown below. Save this program with the name **Project 3-2.cpp**. As you enter the code, add comments in the appropriate places.

```
#include <iostream.h>

main()
{
    float forgnCurr, xRate, dollars;
    char CurrString[15];


    cout << "Enter the amount of money you have in foreign currency:  ";
    cin >> forgnCurr;

    cout << "\nEnter the name of the currency you are converting from:  ";
    cin >> CurrString;

    cout << "\nEnter today's exchange rate for the foreign currency in
        dollars:  ";
    cin >> xRate;

    dollars = forgnCurr * xRate;

    cout << "\nThe amount of " << CurrString << " you have is worth:
        " << dollars << "\n";

    return 0;

}
```

Remember to save your code after typing in the first line or two of your program, and then as often as possible thereafter.

1. List your comments, where they were placed, and explain why.

_____

_____

_____

2. Explain why the float variable type was used for the numeric variables.

_____

Step 4: Save Your Program

Once you have finished typing in the code, save it one final time before compiling your program.

Step 5: Build and Link

Enter the commands necessary to build and link your program. If your program links properly, then **STOP**. If errors occur during any of these processes, check your code, correct any errors, and relink the program.

At this point you should have a working program. Now we need some "real" data in order to run the program.

Step 6: Finding Data

Input the following foreign exchange rates. (*Note:* These are only sample rates. You should be able to find actual, current rates in your local paper, on the Internet, or by calling your local bank.)

CURRENCY	FOREIGN CURRENCY IN $	$ IN FOREIGN CURRENCY
Dollar (Canada)	.6562	1.5239
Yen (Japan)	.008671	115.33
Peso (Mexico)	.100503	9.9500
Mark (Germany)	.6024	1.6601

Step 7: Run Your Program

Now that you have your data ready, run the program on your compiler. When prompted, input the requested information. The program will ask for the amount from the appropriate column.

Just to be sure the program is working properly, check the output against a calculator. If everything checks out, which it should, you have another working program!

PROJECT 3-3:
Dollar to Foreign Currency Conversions

Ⓑ

SCANS

Now, let's see what you've learned. You are going to code this project by yourself. All the information you need has already been presented to you. Follow the steps below and the hints provided to complete this project. Also, make sure you make use of the space provided to list the things you do inside each step.

This project is simple. Instead of converting foreign currency to dollars, you will be converting dollars into a foreign currency. Just think how useful this would be on your next business trip or vacation to some foreign locale!

Step 1: Code the General Outline of the Main()

In the space provided below, outline the code needed for the Main().

_____

_____

_____

_____

_____

_____

Step 2: Start Your Compiler

If your compiler is not running already, start it now.

Step 3: Type in Your Code

You need to write your code before you can type it in. Up to this point you've been given the code to key in. This time, you write the code. In Step 1 you outlined the Main(). Now, design the body of the code. Feel free to look back at previous examples, especially Project 3-2, during this project.

The first thing you should do is lay out the calculation needed for the program. You can do this with a diagram, *flowchart*, or *pseudocode*. Review the last project while observing what the program actually does. Print out the code and take a look at how the program functions as you run it. Your job is to code a program that does the conversion in the opposite direction. Give it some thought.

HOT TIP

If a foreign currency amount multiplied by a conversion rate (foreign currency in dollars) gives you the amount of dollars that the foreign currency is worth, then would it not be true that dollars multiplied by a conversion rate (dollars in foreign currency) would give you the amount of the foreign currency that the dollars are worth?

1.   In the space below, lay out the calculation needed for this project.

_____

Second, you need to identify your variables. You will notice from the code in Project 3-2 that the only variables needed were the ones used in the calculation. These variables were used for input, manipulation, and output. REMEMBER: variable names and type should make sense in regard to the values they will contain and the calculation they will perform. The major difference here will be that the variables need to be named differently. In this case, the type can remain the same.

4 1

2. In the space below, list and name the variables you will use in this program. Explain the data types assigned to each variable.

_____

_____

_____

_____

_____

_____

_____

Third, set up your input and output lines. Remember that your program is working in reverse so the sentences used in your prompts and outputs need to reflect that difference.

3. Edit the code for your 4 cout and 3 cin lines.

cout _____

cin _____

cout _____

cin _____

cout _____

cin _____

cout _____

4. In the space below, organize your code. This way you can input it in the proper order.

_____

_____

_____

_____

_____

_____

_____

_____

_____

_____

_____

_____

_____

_____

_____

_____

_____

_____

_____

_____

_____

_____

_____

_____

_____

_____

_____

5. Type in the code you have developed. Save the file as **Project 3-3.cpp**. Save your code repeatedly after every three or four lines.

Step 4: Save Your Program

Once you have finished typing in your code, save your code one final time before compiling your program.

Step 5: Build and Link

Enter the commands necessary to build and link your program. If your program links properly, then **STOP**. If errors occur during any of these processes, check your code, correct any errors, and re-link the program.

Step 6: Finding Data

Use the same data listed in Step 6 of Project 3-2. Again, you can find current data in your local paper, by calling your local bank, or by searching the Internet.

Step 7: Run Your Program

Now that you have your data ready, run the program on your compiler. When prompted, input the requested information. The program will ask for the amount from the appropriate column.

Just to be sure the program is working properly, check the output against a calculator. If everything checks out, which it should, you have another working program!

In this program, the calculations will be slightly harder. You will convert your height from feet and inches to meters and centimeters. Instead of writing two separate programs as you did earlier, you will include both calculations in the same function.

Very rarely will you write a program that will perform one calculation and then terminate. You may write a *function* that will perform a single calculation, and then return control to the main function or another function. This topic will be expanded on later in this lesson. Start with your multiple-calculation program.

Step 1: Start Your Compiler

If your compiler is not already running, start it now.

Step 2: Type in Your Code

Type in the code as shown below. Save the program as **Project 3-4.cpp**. *Remember:* Save often as you type in the code. Add comments to your code as your enter it.

```cpp
#include <iostream.h>

main()
{
    double centMtr, mtr;
    double inches, tempInches;
    double feet, tempTotal;

    cout << "Enter your height in feet and inches.\t Feet: ";
    cin >> feet;
    cout << "\n\t\t\t\t\t Inches: ";
    cin >> inches;

    tempInches = feet * 12;
    tempTotal = tempInches + inches;
    centMtr = tempTotal * 2.54;

    mtr = centMtr/100;

    cout << "\nYou are " << centMtr << " centimeters tall.\n";
    cout << "\nAnd that converts to " << mtr << " meters tall.\n\n";

    return 0;

}
```

1. List your comments, where they were placed, and explain why.

_____

_____

_____

_____

_____

_____

Step 3: Save Your Program

When you have completed typing the code, save your program once more before moving on to the next step.

Step 4: Build, Link, Run

Enter the commands necessary to build, link, and run your program. If errors occur during any of these processes, check your code, correct any errors, and rerun the program.

Remember to save your program any time you make changes!

When you run your program you will be prompted to enter your height, first in feet and then in inches. When you hit Enter you will have your height calculated in both centimeters and meters.

You now have a program that performs a metric conversion. Additional metric conversion programs will now prove easy to create because all you have to do is rename variables and replace the calculation.

HOT TIP

If you want to convert ONLY inches to centimeters, then enter a 0 for feet and put the total number of inches in when prompted.

Step 5: Explain Your Program

Make sure you keep practicing your ability to analyze and explain C++ code. Explain each line or block of code in the space provided below.

```
#include <iostream.h>
```

_____

```
main()
{
```

_____

_____

```
double centMtr, mtr;
double inches, tempInches;
double feet, tempTotal;
```

_____

_____

```
cout << "Enter your height in feet and inches.\t Feet: ";
cin >> feet;
cout << "\n\t\t\t\t\t Inches: ";
cin >> inches;
```

```
tempInches = feet * 12;
tempTotal = tempInches + inches;
centMtr = tempTotal * 2.54;
```

```
mtr = centMtr/100;
```

```
cout << "\nYou are " << centMtr << " centimeters tall.\n";
cout << "\nAnd that converts to " << mtr << " meters tall.\n\n";
```

```
    return 0;

}
```

When you're finished, compare your answers with those of your teacher and classmates to re-inforce your ability to analyze C++ code.

One additional benefit that hasn't been mentioned involves compounded cout lines like the following.

```
cout << "\nYou are " << centMtr << " centimeters tall.\n";
cout << "\nAnd that converts to " << mtr << " meters tall.\n\n";
```

The benefit of creating a compound cout line such as these, is that the **stream insertion operator** (**<<**) when used multiple times within an output line, **concatenates** the strings within the line.

4 6

PROJECT 3-5:
Short Term Loan/Simple Interest

Ⓑ

The last calculation you will code deals with borrowing short-term money from the bank. Many businesses and individuals borrow various amounts of money for short time periods in order to meet certain financial obligations. They then pay this money back, usually in a number of months, with simple interest added on. Simple interest is interest that is calculated on the principal (the amount borrowed) only; there is no compounding (charging interest on interest) involved as with long-term borrowing.

In this project, we will discuss **precedence**. Precedence is the order in which **arithmetic operators** are applied within a formula. This order is the same as in algebra. Arithmetic operations are performed in the following order:

( )

*, /, or %

+ or -

It's important to know in which order these operators are applied. If you do not pay attention to precedence you will end up with an arithmetic calculation that does *not* do what you expect! Use parentheses to establish which operations are carried out first. Since the operators inside parentheses are applied first, simply use parentheses to segregate the portions of your multiple calculations. Parentheses also help make your code more readable. Anyone looking at code will find it easier to follow if your calculations, at least the harder ones, are segregated with parentheses.

Step 1: Start Your Compiler

If your compiler is not already running, start it now.

Step 2: Type in Your Code

Type in the code as shown below. Save the program as **Project 3-5.cpp**. *Remember:* Save often as you type in the code. Add comments to your code as your enter it.

```cpp
#include <iostream.h>

main()
{
    float principal, intRate, payment;
    float months, period;

    cout << "Enter the amount of money you want to borrow: ";
    cin >> principal;

    cout << "\nEnter the interest percent you will be charged: ";
    cin >> intRate;

    cout << "\nEnter the number of months for which you will borrow the
        money: ";
    cin >> months;
```

4 7

```
    period = months * 30 / 365;
    payment = principal + (principal * ((intRate/100) * period));

    cout << "\nThe total amount of money you will owe in ";
    cout << months << " months will be " << payment << ".\n\n";

    return 0;
}
```

1. List your comments, where they were placed, and explain why.

_____

_____

_____

_____

_____

_____

Step 3: Save Your Program

When you have completed typing the code, save your program once more before moving on to the next step.

Step 4: Build, Link, Run

Enter the commands necessary to build, link, and run your program. If errors occur during any of these processes, check your code, correct any errors, and rerun the program.

Remember to save your program any time you make changes!

When your run your program, you will be prompted to enter the amount you want to borrow (principal), the interest rate you will be charged (for example, 9.75), and the number of months for which you would like to borrow the money. When you press Enter you will be shown the amount of money you will need to pay back to the bank.

Step 5: Explain Your Program

Make sure you keep practicing your ability to analyze and explain C++ code. Let's focus on the line of code shown below containing the calculation:

```
period = months * 30 / 365;
```

Interest rates are technically an annual percentage rate (APR). Because the interest percent you entered is the interest for an entire year, you need to proportion the part of the year for which you borrowed the money. So, in this line of code the number of months you entered is multiplied by 30 and then divided by 365.

If you remember operator precedence, you will know that the * and / operators are at the same level of precedence; therefore, those operations are performed first, beginning at the left.

1. Rewrite this line of code in the space below, using parentheses to make the code easier to read.

_____

Now take a look at the next line:

```
payment = principal + (principal * ((intRate/100) * period));
```

This line of code makes liberal use of parentheses. It may look complicated at first; however, if you break it down one set of parentheses at a time, you will see how easy it is to read.

Start with the innermost set of parentheses: (intRate/100). This portion of the calculation takes the interest rate that you entered and divides it by 100. This converts the interest rate, as you like to see it (for example 9.75), into the decimal equivalent needed by the calculation (.0975).

The next set of parentheses actually includes this one: ((intRate/100) * period). This part of the calculation takes the answer from the first part and multiplies it by the answer from the first line of code you reviewed. If you had actually entered 9.75 as your interest percent, then this line of code would appear as ((.0975) * period).

Next, move to the last set of parentheses: (principal * ((intRate/100) * period)). In this last set of parentheses you are simply multiplying the principal (the amount of money you borrowed) by the answer from your first two sets of parentheses.

Walk through these two lines, up to this point, step by step using actual numbers.

a. If, when asked for the number of months, you had entered the number 3, the first line of code would have calculated the following:

3 * 30 = 90, then 90 / 365 = .2465753 (or an approximate number).

Then the program would have moved on to the next line of code.

b. The first calculation to be performed on the next line would be (intRate/100).

Using the interest rate from the review above, this calculation would perform the following:

9.75 / 100 = .0975

c. The calculation in the second set of parentheses would perform as follows:

.0975 * .2465753 (from the previous line of code) = .0240411

d. The calculation in your last set of parentheses would then multiply your principal by the answer above. If you had borrowed $1,000.00, then the calculation would be performed as follows:

1000 * .0240411 = 24.041096

The two lines of code up to this point have calculated the amount of simple interest you will have to pay back to the bank *in addition* to the amount you borrowed. This leads us to the last calculation on this line: principal + (principal * ((intRate/100) * period)).

e. All you have left to do is to add the amount of interest that you calculated to the amount of money that you borrowed. This last part of the calculation will be performed as follows:

1000 + 24.041096 = 1024.041096

Therefore, if you borrow $1,000.00 from the bank for three months at 9.75%, you will need to repay the bank $1,024.04 three months from the day you borrow the money. As you can see, this program will prove useful to anyone borrowing money for a short period of time.

As mentioned earlier in this lesson, programs usually do not perform one single calculation and then terminate. They usually perform an integrated set of tasks made up of a series of **functions**. A function is a small module of code that usually does one thing. The main function then calls these smaller functions as they are needed. Being **called** by the main, or another, function then performs this function. You are now going to turn your calculations into functions.

When you create a function you need to create a **function prototype**. The function prototype basically makes sure that your compiler knows that the function you are using is valid. Then, inside the program you need to include a **function definition**. The function definition is the actual section of code that performs the function. The function definition and the function prototype need to be exactly the same or the function will not work. The function itself is called, or **invoked**, using the function name. If you have any concerns regarding functions, make sure you review them with your teacher.

The benefits of using functions is that they are small, single-task "mini-programs," they can be reused, and they help decrease the number of comments because they should *all* use meaningful names. Now begin to turn your programs into functions!

Step 1: Start Your Compiler

If your compiler is not already running, start it now.

Step 2: Type in Your Code

Type in the code as shown below. This program is a modification of the miles-to-kilometer project in Lesson 1. Save this program as **Project 3-6.cpp**. *Remember:* Save often as you type in the code. Add the included comments to your code as your enter it.

HOT TIP

Open the **MI to KM.cpp** file, modify the code as shown below, and save it as **Project 3-6.cpp**.

```cpp
// Miles To Kilometer Function Program
// Programmer: <Enter Your Name>

// Include the header file needed for input/output
#include <iostream.h>


//Function Prototype
double MileConvert(double MI);


//Main Function
main()
{
    // Variables are declared
    double miles, kilometers;

    // The user is prompted for input
    cout << "Enter the number of miles you've run:  ";
```

```
    cin >> miles;

    // The function is CALLED and performed returning our answer
    kilometers = MileConvert(miles);


    // Our results are output
    cout <<  miles  <<  " miles is equal to ";
    cout <<  kilometers  <<  " kilometers."  <<  '\n';

    // We end the main function because we are done!
    return 0;

}


//Function definition
double MileConvert(double M)
{

    // The actual function formula
    // and the return that ends this function
    return M / .62;
}
```

Step 3: Save Your Program

When you have completed typing the code, save your program once more before moving on to the next step.

Step 4: Build, Link, Run

Enter the commands necessary to build, link, and run your program. If errors occur during any of these processes, check your code, correct any errors, and rerun the program.

Remember to save your program any time you make changes!

This program should ask for the same information as did the original miles-to-kilometer conversion program. The way the information is processed will be slightly different—and that's what you will focus on.

Step 5: Explain Your Program

1. Define function prototype and explain the purpose a function prototype serves.

_____

_____

_____

_____

5 1

2. Write the line of code that invokes the function. Explain the use of the "miles" variable.

_____

_____

3. Define function definition and explain the purpose of a function definition.

_____

_____

_____

4. Explain what happens when the function is called.

_____

_____

5. Write the line of code that ends the MileConvert function. Explain what the line of code does.

_____

_____

_____

_____

You now have a program that includes a function other than the main function. Upon reviewing the program you may not see a great deal of difference between the original program and the modified one; however, once you begin to add multiple functions you'll see how organized and structured your programs will become.

 **P R O J E C T   3 - 7 : Multiple Functions**

Now take Project 3-4 from earlier in this lesson and modify the code so that you create two separate functions for the conversion into centimeters and meters.

Step 1: Start Your Compiler

If your compiler is not already running, start it now.

Step 2: Type in Your Code

Type in the code as shown below. This program is a modification of the height conversion project you completed

> **HOT TIP**
>
> Open the **Project 3-4.cpp** file, modify the code as shown below, and save as **Project 3-7.cpp**.

earlier in this lesson. Save this program as **Project 3-7.cpp**. *Remember:* Save often as you type in the code. Add the necessary comments to your code as your enter it.

```
#include <iostream.h>

double convertCM(double, double);
double convertMeter(double, double);

main()
{
   double feet, inches;
   double centMtr, mtr;


   cout << "Enter your height in feet and inches.\t Feet: ";
   cin >> feet;
   cout << "\n\t\t\t\t\t Inches: ";
   cin >> inches;

   centMtr = convertCM(feet, inches);
   mtr = convertMeter(feet, inches);


   cout << "\nYou are " << centMtr << " centimeters tall.\n";
   cout << "\nAnd that converts to " << mtr << " meters tall.\n\n";

   return 0;

}

double convertCM(double f, double i)
{
   double tempInches;
   double tempTotal;

   tempInches = f * 12;
   tempTotal = tempInches + i;
   return tempTotal * 2.54;
}

double convertMeter(double f, double i)
{
   double tempInches;
   double tempTotal;

   tempInches = f * 12;
   tempTotal = tempInches + i;
   return (tempTotal * 2.54)/100;
}
```

Step 3: Save Your Program

When you have completed typing the code, save your program once more before moving on to the next step.

Step 4: Build, Link, Run

Enter the commands necessary to build, link, and run your program. If errors occur during any of these processes, check your code, correct any errors, and rerun the program.

Remember to save your program any time you make changes!

This program should ask for the same information as did the original height conversion program. The way the information is processed will be slightly different.

Step 5: Explain Your Program

1. Explain the following line of code.

```
#include <iostream.h>
```

_____

2. What comments did you add to explain this line?

_____

3. Explain the following lines of code.

```
double convertCM(double, double);
double convertMeter(double, double);
```

_____

_____

4. What comments did you add for these lines?

_____

5. Summarize the following block of code.

```
main()
{
   double feet, inches;
   double centMtr, mtr;


   cout << "Enter your height in feet and inches.\t Feet: ";
   cin >> feet;
   cout << "\n\t\t\t\t\t Inches: ";
   cin >> inches;
```

_____

_____

_____

6. What comments did you add for this block of code?

_____

_____

_____

7. Explain the following lines of code.

```
centMtr = convertCM(feet, inches);
mtr = convertMeter(feet, inches);
```

_____

_____

_____

_____

8. What comments did you add for these lines?

_____

9. Summarize the following block of code.

```
cout << "\nYou are " << centMtr << " centimeters tall.\n";
cout << "\nAnd that converts to " << mtr << " meters tall.\n\n";

return 0;

}
```

_____

_____

10. What comments did you add for this block of code?

_____

_____

11. Explain the following lines of code.

```
double convertCM(double f, double i)
{
    double tempInches;
    double tempTotal;

    tempInches = f * 12;
    tempTotal = tempInches + i;
    return tempTotal * 2.54;
}
```

_____

_____

_____

_____

_____

12. What comments did you insert for these lines?

_____

13. Explain the following lines of code.

```
double convertMeter(double f, double i)
{
   double tempInches;
   double tempTotal;

   tempInches = f * 12;
   tempTotal = tempInches + i;
   return (tempTotal * 2.54)/100;
}
```

_____

_____

_____

_____

_____

14. What comments did you insert for these lines?

_____

You now have two separate projects that include the use of functions. As discussed earlier in this Lesson, functions are very useful and are an expected part of good programs. You should begin using functions in all of your multiple function programs.

PROJECT 3-8 : Header Files

Now that you are able to use functions to make your programming life more structured, you need to add one more tidbit to make your functions even more organized. **_Header files_** (.h extension) are used to contain function prototypes as well as definitions of various data types and constants needed by the functions.

You are going to create a simple header file for Project 3-7 using the same code.

Step 1: Start Your Compiler

If your compiler is not already running, start it now.

Step 2: Modify Your Code

Open your **Project 3-7.cpp** file. Type in the following line of code where shown:

```
#include <iostream.h>
#include <Lesson3.h>
```

Cut the following lines of code from this file:

```
double convertCM(double, double);
double convertMeter(double, double);
```

Save your file as **Project 3-8.cpp**.

Create a new text file. Then paste the cut code from Project 3-7 into the new file. It should look exactly like the following:

```
double convertCM(double, double);
double convertMeter(double, double);
```

Save this new file as **Lesson3.h**. You *must* save this file in the same directory that your compiler stores the other .h files. This way when you link your Project 3-8 program, your compiler will be able to find the Lesson3.h file. In Visual C++ 6.0, the .h files are stored in the following directory: \<*system root*>*Program Files\Microsoft Visual Studio\Vc98\Include*. If you do not know where your compiler stores its .h files, ask your instructor.

 HOT TIP

Make sure that you are *not* naming your file with the same name as a header file that is built into your compiler. Obviously, if you do this you will eliminate part of your compiler.

Step 3: Save Both Files

When you have completed typing the code, save both of your files once more before moving on to the next step.

Step 4: Build, Link, Run

Enter the commands necessary to build, link, and run Project 3-8.cpp. If errors occur during any of these processes, check your code, correct any errors, and rerun the program.

Remember to save your program any time you make changes!

This program should ask for the same information as did the original height conversion program. The way the information is processed will once again be slightly different. Instead of the function prototypes being included in the program file (Project 3-8), the prototypes now exist in the Lesson3.h header file. This allows you to accumulate *related* function prototypes into one header file that can be used repeatedly anytime you need to use one of the functions. When you link your program this time, you are now building a link to the Lesson3.h file in addition to the iostream.h file.

You're well on your way to building organized, efficient C++ programs!

Performing Calculations Vs. Storing Values

Should you perform calculations every time you need an answer or should you save the answer for later use? This is a very important issue when performing calculations.

In the Introduction to this lesson, an employee's total hours worked was used as an example. Because the regular hours worked and the overtime hours worked were known, you could calculate the total hours worked rather quickly. Since it was a simple calculation requiring very little processing time, you could probably get away with repeating the calculation every time you wanted the answer.

However, the best way to answer this question overall is to compare processing time to storage space. The question is: Will it be easier on your system to perform the calculation once, and then store the answer? Or will it be easier to perform the calculation every time without storing the answer at all? The answer depends on the system and how the system administrator is trying to optimize the system's performance.

Your job is to make sure your programs help optimize the system or at least run within the established framework. And the best way to do this is to discuss things with your system administrator. In the world of *distributed processing*—computing that takes place on multiple machines in multiple locations—you as a programmer need to be aware of system *infrastructures* and system *capabilities*. Start now in learning about systems by discussing things with your school's system administrator or technology coordinator.

Summary

You focused on calculations in this lesson. You began with a very simple calculation that was basically an output manipulator. Then you moved on to programs that required you to code the actual calculations or conversions. The one important feature of every program is the requirement of collecting data from the user. As a programmer, you will not know the needs of every user; therefore, you need to write your programs so that each user can get the desired solution.

Variables were also stressed: Meaningful variable names, necessary variable types, and the use of variables within the program that the user never sees. These are all very important aspects of making your program readable.

When you moved into complex calculations, precedence was discussed. It's very important that your calculations work correctly. If you are not aware of the order in which operations are carried out, then it is very likely that your calculations will not work correctly. Use parentheses to control the order of operations.

You also learned how to modify programs so that calculations became programs themselves, or functions. Functions allow you to create "mini" programs that can be called by the main function when needed. These calculations can be used repeatedly in whatever program you place them.

And last, but not least, you moved your function prototypes into a header file. Header files take some of the clutter out of your programs by moving function prototypes and data and constant definitions into a separate file. The header files are then attached to the main program by using the #include preprocessor directive.

LESSON 3 REVIEW QUESTIONS

SHORT ANSWER

Define the following in the space provided.

1. Manipulators

2. Objects

3. Hex

4. Oct

5. Preprocessor

6. Flowchart

7. Pseudocode

8. Function

9. Stream insertion operator

10. Concatenates

11. Precedence

12. Arithmetic operators

_____

13. Readability

_____

_____

14. Function prototype

_____

15. Function definition

_____

16. Invoked

_____

17. Header files

_____

_____

18. Called

_____

WRITTEN QUESTIONS

Write your answers to the following questions in the space provided.

1. What is the main purpose of a calculation?

_____

2. Why is it important for calculations to perform correctly?

_____

_____

3. How can flowcharting or pseudocoding be helpful in designing your code?

_____

_____

_____

_____

4. Explain the importance of meaningful variable names.

_____

_____

5. Explain the importance of assigning the correct data type to a variable.

_____

_____

_____

6. Explain the advantage of using the stream insertion operator (<<) multiple times within an output line.

_____

_____

7. List all the arithmetic operators in their order of precedence.

_____

_____

_____

_____

_____

8. Explain the difference between a function prototype and a function definition.

_____

_____

_____

9. Explain the use of header files.

_____

_____

_____

10. What is the "trade-off" when deciding to store data or to simply rerun a calculation every time you need an answer?

_____

_____

_____

Estimated Time:
Application 3-1 30 minutes
Application 3-2 2 hours
Application 3-3 30 minutes

APPLICATION 3-1 ⓑ

In Project 3-5, you created a program that would calculate simple interest on a short-term loan. One alternative that banks give to customers who borrow short-term is to *discount* their loan. This means that the customer allows the bank to subtract the amount of interest from the loan proceeds (the amount of money the customer receives). Then, when customers repay the loan, they only have to repay the amount borrowed. For example, if you were to borrow $1,000 for 12 months at 10% interest, then you would owe the bank $1,100 when you repaid the loan. The interest would be $100. Discounting would allow you to pay the $100 interest upfront. If you chose to do that, then you would only receive $900 from the bank ($1,000 – $100 interest). However, at the end of the 12 months you would only repay the $1,000 since you had already paid the interest.

1. Open the **Project 3-5.cpp** program file.

2. Print out the code to this program.

3. Redesign the calculation so that the interest is subtracted.

4. Add two output lines that tell the borrower how much interest the bank is subtracting and how much the borrower's proceeds are.

5. Save the modified code as **App3-1.cpp**.

APPLICATION 3-2

Create functions for both Project 3-2 and Project 3-3. Since both projects are similar, the work done on one should easily be replicated for the other. Following are suggested steps for doing one of the projects.

1. Open the **Project 3-2.cpp** program file.

2. Run this program with sample data to determine what a correct answer should be.

3. Print out the code to this program.

4. Design the function prototype.

5. Design the function definition.

6. Create the line of code that invokes the function.

7. Modify the original file. Save the modified file as **App3-2.cpp**.

8. Build, link, and run your program. If you encounter errors, review and correct your code.

9. If you encounter no errors, then run your program with the same test data as in Step #2. Compare answers.

10. Create the function for Project 3-3.

APPLICATION 3-3

Move all of the function prototypes you have created for every project or application in this lesson into the Lesson3.h header file. This will include Project 3-6, Application 3-2, and Application 3-3.

1. Open the **Lesson3.h** header file.

2. Enter the prototypes not already in the file.

3. Save the file.

4. Remove the function prototypes from each individual program file. Add the preprocessor directive into each program that will allow the program to link to **Lesson3.h**.

5. Build, link, and run each of the programs to make sure they work correctly.

CRITICAL THINKING   Estimated Time: 4–6 hours

Create a list of calculations that will prove useful to you. In this lesson you will use short-term loan calculations, foreign currency translations, metric conversions, and numbering system conversions. Each profession has calculations that are useful on a daily basis.

Select a group of useful calculations and write code for these calculations. For example, create a file for baseball statistics (batting average, ERA, slugging percentage, fielding percentage) or other sports statistics, grade calculations, exercise/workout records, or anything else of interest to you.

When you are finished writing the code and saving your files, modify each of the programs so that your calculations are converted into functions. If you decide to do so, you may even skip the first step and head right into writing your calculations as functions. However, if you need the practice, write the simple program first, and then convert it into a function.

When you are finished with the functions, create a header file for the function prototypes from all of your functions. Save this header file in the appropriate place for your compiler.

DECISION MAKING

OBJECTIVES

Upon completion of this lesson, you should be able to:

■ Explain control structures.

■ Demonstrate the use of sequence and selection control structures.

■ Discriminate between the use of the if, the if/else, and the switch selection structures.

■ Design code that utilizes the three selection structures.

■ Revise earlier projects by integrating selection structures.

■ Analyze your programs to determine their correctness.

🕐 **Estimated Time: 7 hours**

Introduction

In developing a program, you must give users the opportunity to choose what they need to do with the program. Rarely, if at all, do you encounter a program that allows the user to do just *one* thing. If you think back to Lesson 2, you will remember that you designed screens that allowed the user to interact with your program. The menu screens provided the user with choices. Those user interfaces, however, lacked *functionality*. You will add that functionality in this lesson.

Control structures let you add this type of functionality to user interfaces and to other portions of a program. A control structure is a tool that directs the user to "jump" to other functions and procedures. There are seven types of control structures, which are grouped into three categories: *sequence*, *selection*, and *repetition*.

You're already familiar with sequence programming, in which your instructions are structured in a top-down manner and basically execute one right after another. Repetition will be addressed in Lesson 5. In this lesson, the selection category is addressed.

Think of selection as *decision-making*. You are required to make a choice, or selection. Then based on your selection, the program does something. Another selection would cause the program to do something else. And that's almost all there is to it!

Decision-making, or selection, uses three different structures: *if*, *if/else*, and *switch*. You have used the if structure in earlier lessons, specifically in Project 2-1 and Project 2-1B. If you remember, you used

6 5

five if statements to decide which choice the user was making from a simple menu. Based on the user's choice, something would happen. In these projects it was to add, modify, delete, view/print a record, or to exit the program. You will use the if structure again by expanding your simple menu.

The if/else structure provides a simple "fork in the road" decision. If a condition is true you follow one road. If the condition is false, you take the other road. The switch structure is a multi-selection option. Instead of offering the user two alternate "roads," the switch allows the user to select from many choices.

This lesson will focus on the following:

■ **Control structures and the use of sequence and selection control structures.** You will apply these two types of control structures.

■ **Discriminating between the use of the if, the if/else, and the switch selection structures, and designing code that utilizes them.** You will learn the appropriate uses of the three selection structures, and you will be given the opportunity to design the code necessary to make them work.

■ **Revise earlier projects by integrating selection structures.** As you progress from lesson to lesson, you are adding useful features to your programs. Now it's time to combine the features into cohesive functions, procedures, and programs. For example, you will be modifying your simple menu from Project 2-1 through the use of selection control structures.

■ **Analyze your programs to determine their correctness.** This part of programming never ends. The bottom line is that your programs must work properly. If you continue to develop your understanding of C++ by constantly analyzing your programs, then you will be the better for it in the long run because you will have developed good work habits.

So, get out your road maps, remember how to make decisions, and prepare to have fun!

P R O J E C T   4 - 1 : Simple Menu Review   (B)

Start this project by reviewing your simple menu project from Lesson 2. In that project, you made use of the if structure.

Step 1: Start Your Compiler

Start your compiler if it is not already running. Open **Project 2-1C.cpp** so that you can review the code.

Step 2: Print Out Your Code

Print out the code from Project 2-1C.cpp. You'll use this code because it is the "finished" version of your simple menu. It will be easier to complete this first project by having a hard copy of the code to which you can refer.

Your code should look like the following:

```
// Project 2-1C
// Programmer: (Your Name)
// This program will introduce the basics of creating
// a heading and adding an aesthetic touch to a simple menu.

#include <iostream.h>


// The main function
```

```
main()
{

// Initialize the menu choice variable

int Choice;


// The following creates a heading for our menu.

    cout << "\t\t\t//////////////////////////////\n";
    cout << "\t\t\t/////////  RECORD  /////////////\n";
    cout << "\t\t\t/////////   MENU   ////////////\n";
    cout << "\t\t\t//////////////////////////////\n";

// The following displays your menu choices on the screen

    cout << "\n\t\t\t1) Add A New Record \n";
    cout << "\t\t\t2) Modify An Existing Record \n";
    cout << "\t\t\t3) Delete An Existing Record \n";
    cout << "\t\t\t4) View/Print An Existing Record \n";
    cout << "\t\t\t5) Exit \n";
    cout << "\n\t\t\tPlease Enter Your Choice:   ";

// The cin command accepts the user's choice

    cin >> Choice;

// The following IF statements provide output based on your choice.

    if (Choice == 1)
        cout << "\n\t\t\tYou chose to add a new record.\n\t\t\t";

    if (Choice == 2)
        cout << "\n\t\t\tYou chose to modify a record.\n\t\t\t";

    if (Choice == 3)
        cout << "\n\t\t\tYou chose to delete a record.\n\t\t\t";

    if (Choice == 4)
        cout << "\n\t\t\tYou chose to view/print a record.\n\t\t\t";

    if (Choice == 5)
        cout << "\n\t\t\tYou chose to Exit this menu.\n\t\t\t";

    if ((Choice != 1) && (Choice != 2) && (Choice != 3) && (Choice != 4)
        &&  (Choice != 5))
        cout << "\n\t\t\tYour choice is NOT valid! Please enter a CORRECT
        choice!\n\t\t\t";

// The return statement ends the function.

    return 0;

}
```

If your code does not look like this, make the necessary modification. Then save your program. After saving the program, build, link, and run it, correcting any errors necessary in order for it to run properly. Save the program one final time. Then print out a hard copy.

Step 3: Review Your Code

Concentrate on reviewing the lines of code shown below.

```
if (Choice == 1)
   cout << "\n\t\t\tYou chose to add a new record.\n\t\t\t";

if (Choice == 2)
   cout << "\n\t\t\tYou chose to modify a record.\n\t\t\t";

if (Choice == 3)
   cout << "\n\t\t\tYou chose to delete a record.\n\t\t\t";

if (Choice == 4)
   cout << "\n\t\t\tYou chose to view/print a record.\n\t\t\t";

if (Choice == 5)
   cout << "\n\t\t\tYou chose to Exit this menu.\n\t\t\t";
```

This code is a good example of the if selection structure. Each line is structured the same, the only difference being that each choice will cause something different to happen.

1. Explain, in general, what happens when any of the five lines are executed.

_____

_____

2. Is using the if structure in this way comparable to using the if/else structure? Why or why not?

_____

_____

Now let's take a look at the last line of the if structure.

```
if ((Choice != 1) && (Choice != 2) && (Choice != 3) && (Choice != 4) &&
    (Choice != 5))
cout << "\n\t\t\tYour choice is NOT valid! Please enter a CORRECT
    choice!\n\t\t\t";
```

3. Explain, in general, what happens when this line is executed.

_____

_____

In this sequence, if any line is true, then the attached event happens. You can make this entire sequence execute faster by using **nested** if/else statements. Nested if/else statements make the code execute faster because as soon as one condition proves to be true, the sequence terminates.

4. In the space below, rewrite this entire segment of code using the if/else selection structure. This will be a nested if/else structure because you are testing for multiple occurrences. In the first five lines of code the only changes will occur at the beginning of the line. In the last line, the one that tests for invalid choices, there will be a "major" modification. Save your modified code as **Project 4-1.cpp**.

_____

_____

_____

_____

_____

_____

_____

_____

_____

_____

Step 4: Build, Link, Run

Enter the commands necessary to build, link, and run your program. If errors occur during any of these processes, check your code, correct any errors, and rerun the program.

Step 5: Test Your Program

Now that your program has run successfully, test the logic behind your code by entering various numbers and characters. If your program responds correctly, then your program is correct. If it doesn't, then you need to correct your code and rebuild, relink and rerun the program.

> **HOT TIP**
>
> **Visual C++ 6.0 users:** Instead of clicking on the Build icon every time, you can bypass that step and click on the Link icon. By clicking on the Link icon, the build happens first and will still show any errors. You simply have one less button to click.

Step 6: Review Your Code

Your code should look similar to the following:

```
// Project 4-1
// Programmer: (Your Name)
// This program will introduce the basics of an if/else structure

#include <iostream.h>


// The main function
```

```
main()
{

// Initialize the menu choice variable

int Choice;


// The following creates a heading for our menu.

   cout  << "\t\t\t//////////////////////////////\n";
   cout  << "\t\t\t////////   RECORD  //////////\n";
   cout  << "\t\t\t/////////   MENU  ///////////\n";
   cout  << "\t\t\t//////////////////////////////\n";

// The following displays your menu choices on the screen

   cout << "\n\t\t\t1) Add A New Record \n";
   cout << "\t\t\t2) Modify An Existing Record \n";
   cout << "\t\t\t3) Delete An Existing Record \n";
   cout << "\t\t\t4) View/Print An Existing Record \n";
   cout << "\t\t\t5) Exit \n";
   cout << "\n\t\t\tPlease Enter Your Choice:   ";

// The cin command accepts the user's choice

   cin >> Choice;

// The following IF/ELSE structure provides output based on your choice.
// AND it provides quicker execution because of a possible early exit from
// the choices.

   if (Choice == 1)
      cout << "\n\t\t\tYou chose to add a new record.\n\t\t\t";

   else if (Choice == 2)
      cout << "\n\t\t\tYou chose to modify a record.\n\t\t\t";

   else if (Choice == 3)
      cout << "\n\t\t\tYou chose to delete a record.\n\t\t\t";

   else if (Choice == 4)
      cout << "\n\t\t\tYou chose to view/print a record.\n\t\t\t";

   else if (Choice == 5)
      cout << "\n\t\t\tYou chose to Exit this menu.\n\t\t\t";

   else
      {
         cout << "\n\t\t\tYour choice is NOT valid!\n";
```

```
             cout << "\t\t\tPlease enter a CORRECT choice!\n\n\t\t\t";
     }
// The return statement ends the function.

   return 0;

}
```

1. You will notice that the final statement is simply an **else** statement. Explain why this is not an **else if** statement.

   _____

   _____

2. Explain why this part of the if/else structure places brackets around the commands to be performed.

   _____

3. Explain why you do not need to list all the valid choices as you did when you used the if structure.

   _____

   You now have a working example of an if/else selection structure. You should be able to use this type of structure in appropriate places in all of your programs!

P R O J E C T 4 - 2 : Switch Selection Structure (B)

In this project, you'll modify your simple menu one more time. This time you'll use a **switch** selection structure. Remember that the switch structure is used when you have multiple options from which to choose. Menus are ideal for the switch structure.

   You'll take a look at the switch structure in two different ways. One will be within the current menu code, and the other will be by redefining your menu components.

Step 1: Start Your Compiler

Start your compiler if it is not already running.

Step 2: Modify Your Code

Open the **Project 4-1.cpp** file. Save it as **Project 4-2.cpp**. Modify the code exactly as shown below. Remember to save your code as you modify it.

```
// Project 4-2
// Programmer: (Your Name)
// This program will introduce the basics of a switch structure

#include <iostream.h>
```

```
// The main function

main()
{

// Initialize the menu choice variable

int Choice;


// The following creates a heading for our menu.

    cout  << "\t\t\t/////////////////////////////\n";
    cout  << "\t\t\t///////   RECORD   ///////////\n";
    cout  << "\t\t\t///////////  MENU   //////////\n";
    cout  << "\t\t\t/////////////////////////////\n";

// The following displays your menu choices on the screen

    cout << "\n\t\t\t1) Add A New Record \n";
    cout << "\t\t\t2) Modify An Existing Record \n";
    cout << "\t\t\t3) Delete An Existing Record \n";
    cout << "\t\t\t4) View/Print An Existing Record \n";
    cout << "\t\t\t5) Exit \n";
    cout << "\n\t\t\tPlease Enter Your Choice:  ";

// The cin command accepts the user's choice

    cin >> Choice;

// The following SWITCH structure provides output based on your choice.
// AND it provides quicker execution because of an early exit when
// the correct choice is made.

    switch (Choice)
    {
            case 1:
                    cout << "\n\t\t\tYou chose to add a new
                            record.\n\t\t\t";
                    break;

            case 2:
                    cout << "\n\t\t\tYou chose to modify a
                            record.\n\t\t\t";
                    break;

            case 3:
                    cout << "\n\t\t\tYou chose to delete a
                            record.\n\t\t\t";
                    break;

            case 4:
```

```
                              cout << "\n\t\t\tYou chose to view/print a
                                      record.\n\t\t\t";
                    break;

            case 5:
                    cout << "\n\t\t\tYou chose to Exit this
                                    menu.\n\t\t\t";
                    break;

            default:
                    cout << "\n\t\t\tYour choice is NOT valid!\n";
                    cout << "\t\t\tPlease enter a CORRECT
                                    choice!\n\n\t\t\t";
    }

// The return statement ends the function.

    return 0;

}
```

Step 3: Build, Link, and Run

Enter the commands necessary to build, link, and run your program. If errors occur during any of these processes, check your code, correct any errors, and recompile the program.

Test your program by selecting all the valid choices and by making a few invalid choices.

Step 4: Review Your Code

Let's take a look at the entire switch structure since it is very similar from line to line.

```
switch (Choice)
{
        case 1:
                cout << "\n\t\t\tYou chose to add a new
                                record.\n\t\t\t";
                break;

        case 2:
                cout << "\n\t\t\tYou chose to modify a
                                record.\n\t\t\t";
                break;

        case 3:
                cout << "\n\t\t\tYou chose to delete a
                                record.\n\t\t\t";
                break;

        case 4:
                cout << "\n\t\t\tYou chose to view/print a
                                record.\n\t\t\t";
                break;
```

```
            case 5:
                    cout << "\n\t\t\tYou chose to Exit this
                            menu.\n\t\t\t";
                    break;

            default:
                    cout << "\n\t\t\tYour choice is NOT valid!\n";
                    cout << "\t\t\tPlease enter a CORRECT
                            choice!\n\n\t\t\t";
}
```

1. The keyword switch is followed by your input variable, Choice. Choice contains the user's menu selection. What does the switch keyword do with the value in the Choice variable?

   _____

   _____

2. Explain why braces enclose all the case options.

   _____

3. Explain the purpose of the case labels.

   _____

   Note the colon, instead of the semicolon, at the end of each case label. This is the proper syntax for the case label line. Also note that the lines to be performed, dependent on the case, *do* end with a semicolon.

4. Default is a special case. Explain the purpose of the default case.

   _____

   One last thing to notice is the default case section of the switch structure. The braces required by compound command lines used in the if/else structure are not required in the case of a switch structure.

   Now that you have used all three selection structures with your menu, there's one last question that needs to be answered.

5. Which of the three selection structures is the most appropriate to use with a menu? Why?

   _____

   _____

   _____

PROJECT 4-3 : Branching Off of Your Menu

Now it's your turn to exhibit some independence. You are going to code parts of this project by yourself. All the code and the hints you need have been presented to you. Follow the steps below and the hints provided to complete this project. Also, make sure you make use of the space provided to list the things you do inside each step.

In this project, you will take your enhanced menu, the one that uses the switch selection structure, and link to the data input screen from Project 2-2. This way when you select the first choice on the enhanced menu you will actually link, or transfer, to the Data Input Screen. So let's get started.

Step 1: Start Your Compiler

Start your compiler if it is not already running.

Step 2: Open the Project 2-2.cpp File

Open the code file for **Project 2-2.cpp**. Save it as **Project 4-3.cpp**.

Step 3: Modify Your Code

You will modify the code by adding a **void** function. A void function is one with an empty parameter list, or one that does *not* return a value. The function prototype looks like this:

```
void functionName();
```

1. Using the above example as a hint, create a function prototype for your Data Input Screen. Write your function prototype in the space below.

_____

_____

_____

2. Now you need to rearrange your code into the main function and the data input function. Use the cut and paste features of your compiler or text editor. Plan your function definition in the space below. You may want to print a copy of your existing code so you can plot your modification easier.

_____

_____

_____

_____

_____

_____

_____

_____

_____

_____

_____

_____

_____

_____

_____

_____

_____

_____

_____

_____

_____

_____

_____

_____

_____

_____

_____

_____

_____

_____

3. Once you've removed the major portion of the code from the main function you need to re-place it with the function call. Write the function call in the space below.

_____

4. Once you have modified your code to create the function for the data input screen, you need to input the changes. Remember to save your changes frequently while typing in your code.

5. When you have made all your changes, build, link, and run the program to make sure it functions properly. If you have build or link errors, correct them and rerun your program. Make sure you save your corrections! When the code is correct, your program should run exactly like it did in Project 2-2.

If you are having major problems at this point, check your code against the code shown below.

```
// Project 4-3 (Was Project 2-2)
// Programmer: <Your Name Here>
// This program will show the design of a data input screen
// using a void function for the input screen code.

// Include the header file necessary for input and output.

#include <iostream.h>

// function prototype
void dataInput();
```

```cpp
// The main function begins.

main()
{
    // The function call
    dataInput();

    // This was used as a test check
    cout <<  "\nWe're back in main!\n";

    return 0;
}

// function definition
void dataInput()
{

    // Initialize the necessary variables.

    char fname[20];        // First Name
    char mi[1];            // Middle Initial
    char lname[30];        // Last Name
    char phnum[7];         // Phone Number not including area code
    char dob[10];          // Date of Birth, Format MM/DD/YYYY
    char email[30];        // E-mail address


    // Set up the input screen
    // Create the Heading

    cout << "\t\t\t%%%%%%%%%%%%%%%%%%%%%%%%%%%%\n";
    cout << "\t\t\t%%%%%% Contact Name %%%%%%\n";
    cout << "\t\t\t%%%%%%%%%%% and %%%%%%%%%%%\n";
    cout << "\t\t\t%%%%%%%%% Address %%%%%%%%%\n";
    cout << "\t\t\t%%%%%%%%%%%%%%%%%%%%%%%%%%%%\n";

    // Inform the user as to what this screen is to be used for.

    cout << "\n\n\tUse this screen to input a new contact to your Personal
            Phone Book.\n";

    // Get the user to enter information.

    cout << "\n\nEnter Contact's First Name:\t";
    cin >> fname;

    cout << "\nEnter Contact's Middle Initial:\t";
    cin >> mi;

    cout << "\nEnter Contact's Last Name:\t";
    cin >> lname;

    cout << "\nEnter Contact's Phone Number\n";
```

```
        cout << "(without the area code):\t";
        cin >> phnum;

        cout << "\nEnter Contact's Date of Birth:\n";
        cout << "(use MM/DD/YYYY format):\t";
        cin >> dob;

        cout << "\nEnter Contact's E-Mail Address:\t";
        cin >> email;

        cout << "\nThe data was input successfully\n";

        // Notice that you do not have to return anything.
}
```

If your code differs, but your program works—that's great! Not all programs that work the same are coded the same.

Step 4: Copy Your Function

Copy your new function to Project 4-2. Before opening Project 4-2, copy the function definition from Project 4-3 onto the Clipboard. Or if you can, simply keep Project 4-3 open as you open Project 4-2.

1. Paste your function definition into the proper place in Project 4-2. In the space below, write the line of code it should appear after.

_____

_____

_____

_____

2. Either type in, or copy and paste, the function prototype and the function call into the proper place in the program. In the space below, write the line of code that the prototype and the call follow.

_____

_____

_____

_____

_____

_____

Save your program as **Project 4-2A.cpp**.

Step 5: Build, Link, Run

Enter the commands necessary to build, link, and run the program. If errors occur during any of these processes, check your code, correct any errors, and relink the program.

Save your modifications before continuing.

Step 6: Testing Your Program

Run your program and see what happens when you choose choice #1, Add A New Record. Your program should work, but the Add A New Record screen begins immediately below the Menu screen. Obviously, that is not what should occur. All the other choices should continue to work as they have before.

You'll need to add a function that clears your monitor before running the Add A New Record screen.

Step 7: Clear Your Screen

In most C/C++ compilers there is not a true "clear screen" function built-in. The clear screen functions are dependent on the compiler and the operating system being used. So, you will create a "pseudo" clear screen function.

You will create a simple function that prints blank lines. The program will use the repetition structure, **while**, to create a **loop** for the lines to print within. You will concentrate on repetitions in the next lesson. However, since the while structure proves to be useful in this situation, here's an explanation of what it does for you.

1. Modify your code from Project 4-2A.cpp so that it includes the new function prototype, the new function definition, and the new function call as shown below. Then, save it as **Project 4-2A**.

```
// Project 4-2A Including the new clearScreen function
// Programmer: (Your Name)
// This program will add the Data Input function
// to the basic switch structure

#include <iostream.h>

// Includes the function prototypes needed for this Lesson
#include <Lesson4.h>


// The main function

main()
{

// Initialize the menu choice variable

int Choice;


// The following creates a heading for our menu.

   cout << "\t\t\t///////////////////////////////\n";
   cout << "\t\t\t////////  RECORD  /////////\n";
   cout << "\t\t\t/////////  MENU  //////////\n";
   cout << "\t\t\t///////////////////////////////\n";

// The following displays your menu choices on the screen
```

```cpp
        cout << "\n\t\t\t1) Add A New Record \n";
        cout << "\t\t\t2) Modify An Existing Record \n";
        cout << "\t\t\t3) Delete An Existing Record \n";
        cout << "\t\t\t4) View/Print An Existing Record \n";
        cout << "\t\t\t5) Exit \n";
        cout << "\n\t\t\tPlease Enter Your Choice:  ";

// The cin command accepts the user's choice

    cin >> Choice;

// The following SWITCH structure provides output based on your choice.
// AND it provides quicker execution because of an early exit when
// the correct choice is made.

    switch (Choice)
    {
        case 1:
                clearScreen();
                dataInput();
                break;

        case 2:
                cout << "\n\t\t\tYou chose to modify a record.\n\t\t\t";
                break;

        case 3:
                cout << "\n\t\t\tYou chose to delete a record.\n\t\t\t";
                break;

        case 4:
                cout << "\n\t\t\tYou chose to view/print a record.\n\t\t\t";
                break;

        case 5:
                cout << "\n\t\t\tYou chose to Exit this menu.\n\t\t\t";
                break;

        default:
                cout << "\n\t\t\tYour choice is NOT valid!\n";
                cout << "\t\t\tPlease enter a CORRECT choice!\n\n\t\t\t";
    }

// The return statement ends the function.

    return 0;

}


// function definitions
```

```
void clearScreen()
{
    int lines = 0;

    while (lines <= 15)
    {
        cout << endl;
        ++lines;
    }
}


void dataInput()
{

// Initialize the necessary variables.

    char fname[20];        // First Name
    char mi[1];            // Middle Initial
    char lname[30];        // Last Name
    char phnum[7];         // Phone Number not including area code
    char dob[10];          // Date of Birth, Format MM/DD/YYYY
    char email[30];        // E-mail address



    // Set up the input screen
    // Create the Heading

    cout << "\t\t\t%%%%%%%%%%%%%%%%%%%%%%%%%%%%\n";
    cout << "\t\t\t%%%%%% Contact Name %%%%%%\n";
    cout << "\t\t\t%%%%%%%%%%% and %%%%%%%%%%%\n";
    cout << "\t\t\t%%%%%%%%%% Address %%%%%%%%%%\n";
    cout << "\t\t\t%%%%%%%%%%%%%%%%%%%%%%%%%%%%\n";

    // Inform the user as to what this screen is to be used for.

    cout << "\n\n\tUse this screen to input a new contact to your Personal
            Phone Book.\n";

    // Get the user to enter information.

    cout << "\n\nEnter Contact's First Name:\t";
    cin >> fname;

    cout << "\nEnter Contact's Middle Initial:\t";
    cin >> mi;

    cout << "\nEnter Contact's Last Name:\t";
    cin >> lname;

    cout << "\nEnter Contact's Phone Number\n";
    cout << "(without the area code):\t";
```

```
        cin >> phnum;

        cout << "\nEnter Contact's Date of Birth:\n";
        cout << "(use MM/DD/YYYY format):\t";
        cin >> dob;

        cout << "\nEnter Contact's E-Mail Address:\t";
        cin >> email;

        cout << "\nThe data was input successfully\n";

        // Notice that we do not have to return anything.
}
```

2. Build, link, and run your program. Correct any errors if necessary, then recompile it. Remember to save your corrected code.

3. Run your program and test the various choices to make sure it functions properly.

> **HOT TIP**
>
> If you haven't noticed, you will need to create a Lesson4.h file to hold the function prototypes. If you choose not to do this, then simply include the function prototypes in with the code.

You will notice that the Add A New Record input screen starts part way down the page. Ignore that for now. As long as your program runs, you've done your job. In order to reposition the cursor you would need to find C++ libraries specific to your compiler, or use BIOS function calls, to make it work properly. For you to implement the proper clear screen method in your version of these projects, you will need to get the proper coding from your instructor. If you are using the South-Western text, *Introduction To Computer Science Using C++,* by Todd Knowlton, you can visit the following Web site for clear screen information: *http://www.ProgramCPP.com,* and the topic is *6.2.1.*

P R O J E C T   4 - 4 : If/Else with Existing Programs

In this project, you will create an if/else selection structure within a program that will allow the user to choose between borrowing money for a period of months or a period of years.

Step 1: Start Your Compiler

If your compiler is not already running, start it now.

Step 2: Design Your Program

Using the code from *Project 3-5* as a basis, design a modified program that gives the user the choice to borrow for either months *or* years. Use an if/else structure that you will build right into the program.

1. In the space below, write the code changes that need to occur. Remember to make note of where they are at in the body of the program. *Remember:* Everywhere you input or output a value pertaining to month now also needs to pertain to years.

_____
_____
_____
_____
_____
_____
_____
_____
_____
_____
_____
_____
_____
_____
_____

Step 3: Type in Your Program

Type in the code as you've modified it. Save the program as **Project 4-4.cpp**. _Remember:_ Save often as you type in the code. Add comments to your code as you enter it.

Step 4: Save Your Program

When you have completed typing the code, save your program once more before moving on to the next step.

Step 5: Build, Link, Run

Enter the commands necessary to build, link, and run your program. If errors occur during any of these processes, check your code, correct any errors, and rerun the program.

Remember to save your program any time you make changes!

Test your program by running calculations in months and then running the same calculations in equivalent periods of years. For example, start with $1,000 at 10% for 12 months. Then compare it to $1,000 at 10% for 1 year. The answers should be comparable.

You now have a program that provides a valuable choice to your users. Although most loans for more than one year are charged compound interest, you can at least make an educated choice at a "ballpark" borrowing cost.

Step 6: Explain Your Program

Make sure you keep practicing your ability to analyze and explain C++ code. Explain each line or block of code from your program in the space provided below.

_____
_____
_____
_____
_____

_____

_____

_____

_____

_____

_____

_____

_____

_____

_____

_____

_____

_____

_____

_____

_____

_____

_____

_____

_____

_____

_____

_____

_____

_____

_____

_____

_____

_____

_____

_____

When you're finished, discuss your answers with your teacher and classmates to reinforce your ability to analyze C++ code.

In this last program you will deal with choosing between different types of financial transactions. You will use a switch selection structure for the main part of the program and then you will include the Project 4-4 if/else structure.

Step 1: Start Your Compiler

If your compiler is not already running, start it now.

Step 2: Design Your Program

Using the code from Project 4-4, and both the **Project 3-3.cpp** (dollar to foreign currency), and the **Project 3-2.cpp** (foreign currency to dollar) conversion projects, design your modified program. You'll want to give the user the choice of which financial program to run. If the user chooses the simple loan calculation, then he or she will have another choice to make.

To increase the challenge of this project, have the selection structure call the chosen calculation as a function for each menu choice.

1. In the space below, write the code needed for your new program. You may want to print hard copies of the necessary programs in order to review what you've done before.

> **HOT TIP**
>
> Outline your main function, set up the program flow, create the function prototypes, then cut and paste the code needed for your functions from the other projects.

_____

_____

_____

_____

_____

_____

_____

_____

_____

_____

_____

_____

_____

_____

_____

_____

_____

_____

_____

_____

_____

_____

_____

_____

_____

_____

_____

_____

_____

Step 3: Type in Your Program

Type in the code as you create each section. Save the program as **Project 4-5.cpp**. _Remember:_ Save often as you type in the code. Add comments to your code as you enter it.

Step 4: Save Your Program

When you have completed typing the code, save your program once more before moving on to the next step.

Step 5: Build, Link, Run

Enter the commands necessary to build, link, and run your program. If errors occur during any of these processes, check your code, correct any errors, and rerun the program.

Remember to save your program any time you make changes!

When you run your program you will need to test the main "menu" for proper switching. You will also need to test each function to make sure the calculations are correct.

Step 6: Explain Your Program

Make sure you keep practicing your ability to analyze and explain C++ code. Explain each line or block of code from your program in the space provided below.

_____

_____

_____

_____

_____

_____

_____

_____

_____

_____

_____

_____

_____

_____

_____

_____

_____

_____

_____

_____

_____

_____

_____

_____

_____

_____

_____

_____

_____

_____

_____

_____

_____

When you're finished, discuss your answers with your teacher and classmates to reinforce your ability to analyze C++ code.

If you are having major problems at this point, check your code against the code shown below.

```cpp
#include <iostream.h>

void dollrConvert();
void forgnConvert();
void simplLoan();

main()
{
   int select;

   cout << "Select the financial calculation you would like to peform.\n";
   cout << "A - Dollar To Foreign Currency Conversion.\n";
   cout << "B - Foreign Currency to Dollar Conversion.\n";
   cout << "C - Simple Loan Calculation.\n";
   cout << "  (The term can be calculated in either months or years)\n";
   cout << "\nEnter Your Selection:  ";
   select = cin.get();

   switch (select)
   {
   case 'A':
   case 'a':
      dollrConvert();
      break;

   case 'B':
   case 'b':
      forgnConvert();
      break;

   case 'C':
   case 'c':
      simplLoan();
      break;

   default:
      cout << "Incorrect Selection.";
      break;
   }

   return 0;
}


void dollrConvert()
{
   float dollars;
   float xRate;
   float answer;
   char CurrString[15];
```

```cpp
    cout << "Enter the amount of money you have in dollars and cents:   ";
    cin >> dollars;

    cout << "\nEnter the name of the currency you need to convert into:   ";
    cin >> CurrString;

    cout << "\nEnter today's exchange rate for the dollar in the foreign
             currency:   ";
    cin >> xRate;

    answer = dollars * xRate;

    cout << "\nThe amount of " << CurrString << " your dollars are worth is:
             " << answer << "\n";

}


void forgnConvert()
{
    float forgnCurr, xRate, dollars;
    char CurrString[15];


    cout << "Enter the amount of money you have in foreign currency:   ";
    cin >> forgnCurr;

    cout << "\nEnter the name of the currency you are converting from:   ";
    cin >> CurrString;

    cout << "\nEnter today's exchange rate for the foreign currency in
             dollars:   ";
    cin >> xRate;

    dollars = forgnCurr * xRate;

    cout << "\nThe amount of " << CurrString << " you have is worth:   " <<
             dollars << "\n";

}


void simplLoan()
{
    int Choice;
    float principal, intRate, payment;
    float time, period;

    cout << "Enter the amount of money you want to borrow: ";
    cin >> principal;
```

```
        cout << "\nEnter the interest percent you will be charged: ";
        cin >> intRate;

        cout << "\nEnter the term for which you will borrow the money: \n";
        cout << "For Months - Enter 1\n";
        cout << "For Years - Enter 2\n";
        cout << "Enter your choice: ";
        cin >> Choice;

        if ( Choice == 1 )
            cout  << "\nEnter the number of months for which you will borrow the
                       money: ";
        else
        cout << "\nEnter the number of years for which you will borrow the money:
";

        cin >> time;

        if ( Choice == 1 )
            period = time * 30 / 365;
        else
            period = time * 365 / 365;

        payment = principal + (principal * ((intRate/100) * period));

        cout << "\nThe total amount of money you will owe in ";

        if ( Choice == 1 )
            cout << time << " months will be  " << payment << ".\n\n";
        else
            cout << time << " years will be  " << payment << ".\n\n";

}
```

Two differences that should be pointed out in this switch selection structure is the cin.get() and the case testing for both upper and lower case. The cin.get() takes the character input from the keyboard and places it in an integer variable. This allows you to read characters as integers. More importantly, it will allow the cin.get() to compare against an end-of-file character for repetition termination. This will be addressed in the next lesson.

The case comparison for both upper and lower case is necessary because who knows what the user will enter—an "A" is the same as an "a" in most users' minds. However, the computer knows there's a difference, so it's your job to make life easier for the user. That's why you test for both type letters.

You now have a program that uses multiple selection structures. You can use these with any of the programs that you have developed so far, whether with this book or elsewhere. So go forth and integrate selection structures where necessary into your code!

Summary

Control structures are a very important part of programming. They allow you to organize programs and to provide control as to the function of the program. They let you provide the user with options and then control how the options are performed. This lesson contained sequence and selection structures and even briefly introduced a repetition structure.

Sequence is simply programming in a top-down structured manner, which C++ does by default. Selection provides users with the ability to choose the functions they would like to perform. It provides the programmer with a way to give the users choices while maintaining control over what happens when they make those choices. Review your code to look for the following: providing the user a selection of choices and then having many instructions performed for users "behind the scenes." This is "control," and it occurs in every program.

In this lesson, you also explored the if, if/else, and switch selection structures. The if structure is the simplest. *If* a condition is true, then something happens. And multiple if statements can be linked together. As mentioned earlier in this lesson, each if statement is tested. Even if the first one is found to be true, the others are tested. This doesn't matter in small programs, but it will in larger ones.

You learned that if/else structures are more efficient than the if statements alone, because once one is found to be true the others are ignored. Another difference between the two structures is the number of choices to be made. The if statement is probably more suitable for a simple two-choice selection; whereas the if/else structure is ideal for multiple selections. You can also link multiple if/else statements and you can include multiple commands under each one. Just remember that braces { } must surround multiple commands under each if/else statement.

The last selection structure is the switch. The switch is neat, organized, and efficient. Although it requires extra commands (case, default, break) and you need to be careful about the syntax (case 'C':), the switch structure is much more organized. Like the if/else structure, once a correct case is encountered, the comparisons stop. But unlike the if/else, multiple commands do *not* need to be placed in braces.

You also got a sneak peek of the while command. When you did your Clear Screen function, you used this command to create a repetition, or loop, that printed a multiple number of lines to the screen. Repetition structures will allow you to get even more creative and to provide more control over your programs.

LESSON 4 REVIEW QUESTIONS

SHORT ANSWER

Define the following in the space provided.

1. if

_____

_____

2. if/else

_____

_____

3. switch

_____

_____

4. Functionality

_____

5. Control structures

_____

6. Sequence

_____

_____

7. Selection

_____

8. Repetition

_____

9. Decision making

_____

10. Nested

_____

_____

11. Void function

_____

12. while

_____

13. Loop

_____

14. case

_____

15. break

_____

16. Hard copy

_____

17. Control

_____

WRITTEN QUESTIONS

Write your answers to the following questions in the space provided.

1. Why do you use control structures?

   _____

   _____

2. Explain how C++ automatically provides you with the sequence control structure.

   _____

   _____

3. Explain the importance of decision making in your programs.

   _____

   _____

4. Explain the difference between the if, if/else, and switch selection structures.

   _____

   _____

   _____

   _____

   _____

5. Give an appropriate example of where to use each of the selection structures.

   _____

   _____

   _____

   _____

6. Write one if/else statement and one switch case statement that performs compound commands. Explain the difference in the syntax.

   _____

   _____

   _____

7. Research and explain the cin.get() function used in Project 4.5.

8. Explain, in general, repetition structures.

9. Explain the difference between the = operator and the = = operator. Refer to Projects 4-1 and 4-5.

10. Explain the following case comparison:

```
case 'A':
case 'a':
   dollrConvert();
   break;
```

TESTING YOUR SKILLS

 **Estimated Time:**

APPLICATION 4-1A

Application 4-1A	45 minutes
Application 4-1B	1 ^{1}/$_4$ hours
Application 4-1C	20 minutes
Application 4-1D	1 ^{1}/$_2$ hours

Create a simple choice list that will allow the user to choose between various conversions. The conversion choices that you will present to the user are from the following projects and applications:

Integer conversion—**Project 3-1** (program)

Distance conversion—**Project 3-6**—Miles to Kilometers (function), and **Application 1-1**—Kilometers to Miles (program)

Temperature conversion—**Critical Thinking** from Lesson 1 (program)

Height conversion—**Project 3-7**—Height To Centimeter/Meter (function)

Use a switch selection structure to allow the program to branch into the various conversions. Also include an Exit choice.

1. Design your screen layout on a piece of paper.

2. Organize only the main choices to be made. For example, once you branch into the distance conversion, the user will have another choice to make.

3. Make a list of the variables you will need.

4. Code the design to the screen layout. Do not initially add the code that will cause your program to branch to the actual routines or functions. Instead, branch to an output line that shows that your selection structure works.

5. Build, link, and run your program.

6. Save the modified code as **App4-1.cpp**.

APPLICATION 4-1B

Create functions for the projects and applications from the list in Application 4-1 that are *not* functions. You will find selection structures much easier to work with if the choices call functions.

1. Create functions for each of the following:

   Project 3-1—Integer conversion (Save as: **App4-1B1**)

   Project 3-6—Miles to Kilometers conversion (Save as: **App4-1B2**)

   Application 1-1—Kilometers to Miles conversion (Save as: **App4-1B3**)

   Project 3-7—Height conversion (Save as: **App4-1B4**)

   Chapter 1 Critical Thinking—Both Fahrenheit to Celsius and the reverse conversion

2. Test each function to make sure that it works properly.

APPLICATION 4-1C

Move all of the function prototypes you have created for every project or application used in this lesson into the Lesson4.h header file. This will include all the prototypes from the lesson itself, plus all the ones used in Application 4-1A and Application 4-1B. If you have not created the Lesson4.h file, create it now.

1. Open the **Lesson4.h** header file.

2. Enter the prototypes not already in the file.

3. Save the file in the proper folder so that your compiler can find it.

4. Add the preprocessor line to your App4-1.cpp program.

APPLICATION 4-1D

Add the function calls and the function definitions to your simple choice list in your App4-1.cpp program.

1. Open your **App4-1.cpp** file and save it as **App4-1 Final**.

2. Add the Integer Conversion function call and definition to your simple choice list.

3. Add the Height Conversion function call and definition to your simple choice list.

At this point you will encounter a slight amount of additional work. Both the Distance Conversions and the Temperature Conversions have two possible choices. You must create simple choice lists for both of these. The narrative below will provide you with two methods for creating an additional choice list. This can be used for both the lists you need to create.

Method A—Code a routine into the switch choice.

1. Inside the case comparison, add a cout line that asks the user to make a choice.

2. Have the user input the choice.

3. Do an if or if/else structure to branch to one or the other function.

4. The pseudocode would look like this:

```
Case 'A':
Case 'a':
     Which of the following would you like to do?
     Enter choice
     If 1 do that choice
     Else do the other
     Break;
```

Method B—Create a selection function.

1. Turn the following pseudocode into a small function. Remember to add the prototype to the Lesson4.h file.

```
void choice()
{
     Which of the following would you like to do?
     Enter choice
     If 1 do that choice
     Else do the other
}
```

2. In this case you would simply add the function call to the case comparison inside the switch selection structure.

Add these new function calls and the function definitions to your simple choice list in your App4-1.cpp program.

Run your App4-1 program to make sure everything functions properly. If not, debug your code and recompile until your entire program functions properly.

Take the group of calculation programs/functions that you created in the Critical Thinking section of Lesson 3. Create a menu that will list the various functions, or groups of functions, from which a user can choose. Implement a selection structure to handle the main menu selections and any nested options that you may need. It's your choice as to which selection structure to use. However, try to use the appropriate structure for each situation.

Then write the remainder of the code necessary (or copy and paste) to create a single program that will allow the user to perform the various calculations you have created.

When you finish this assignment, you will have a complete multiple-selection program to call your own! Think portfolio!

REPETITIONS

Upon completion of this lesson, you should be able to:

■ Demonstrate the use of repetition control structures.

■ Discriminate between the use of the **while**, the **do/while**, and the **for** repetition structures.

■ Design code that utilizes the three repetition structures.

■ Revise earlier projects by integrating repetition structures.

■ Analyze your programs to determine their correctness.

⏱ **Estimated Time: 7 hours**

Introduction

One of the strengths of computers is their ability to perform calculations at a tremendously fast speed. Because of that ability it makes sense to let them perform calculations that would take human beings a great deal of time to finish. A great many times these calculations must be repeated again and again to arrive at the correct answer, such as in the case of compound interest. That is why *repetition control structures* are used.

Repetition control structures allow you to add *looping* to your programs. Looping simply means that a sequence of code is repeated over and over, until a condition is met. However, there is a danger with repetition control structures that the looping will get out of hand and create an "endless" loop. This means that you have provided a condition, or coded your logic wrong, so that the ending condition will never be met.

You'll find that repetition is very useful in the programs you write. For example, the data input function you developed in Project 4-2 allows the user to enter data into an address book. The way the program operates now, the user enters one record and then the program ends. In order to input another record, the program must run again. This is not very efficient. It makes more sense to let the user enter records until he or she is finished.

As mentioned in Lesson 4, there are seven types of control structures that are grouped into three categories: *sequence*, *selection*, and *repetition*. This lesson covers the repetition category.

There are three repetition control structures, *while*, *do/while*, and *for*. The differences between the three are subtle, but necessary to understand. The *while* structure is built on the premise that the commands in the body of the while structure will continue to execute "while" some condition is true. When the condition becomes false, the while structure releases control and executes the next line after the while structure. The condition is tested for at the beginning of the structure. This means that there is a possibility that the while structure may not even be entered if the condition is not met. Also, make note that the commands in the body of the while structure must be surrounded by braces.

In a *do/while* structure, the commands are executed until the while condition becomes false; however, the while condition is tested for after the command(s) executes. This means that the commands will execute *at least once*. This is very useful if the user chooses to do something, but only needs to perform the action one time. The commands in the do/while structure are also enclosed in braces; however, the commands are part of the *do* section of the structure.

Last, but not least is the *for* structure. The syntax of this structure is slightly more complicated, but easy to understand once you see it. The for structure uses a **counter** to control repetition. The format of the for structure causes a counter to be initialized to a specific value, a condition for the counter to be measured against is then created, and then an action takes place, usually an **increment** of the counter. The following is an example of the for structure:

```
for ( int counter =1; counter <= 10; counter++)
    cout << "This is a for structure.\n";
```

In this example, the variable counter is initialized to the number 1. This loop will execute as long as the counter is less than or equal to 10, and after each loop the counter will be incremented by 1 after the command executes. By placing this structure into a program you will get a screen filled with 10 separate lines of "This is a for structure." You will get the opportunity to code all three structures plus some variations.

This lesson will focus on the following:

- **Control structures and the use of repetition control structures.** You will learn about repetition control structures, and understand when and how to apply them, as well as other types of control structures.

- **When to use the while, the do/while, and the for repetition structures and designing code that utilizes each.** You will learn the appropriate use of the three repetition structures, and you will be given the opportunity to design the code necessary to make them work.

- **Revising earlier projects by integrating repetition structures.** You will modify code you've already created by integrating repetition structures.

- **Analyze your programs to determine their correctness.** This part of programming never ends. The bottom line is that your programs must work properly. If you continue to develop your understanding of C++ by constantly analyzing your programs, then you will be the better for it in the long run because you will have developed good work habits!

So, get out your hula hoops and get ready to loop!

PROJECT 5-1 : Simple Repetition Overview

Start this project by doing a simple comparison between the three repetition structures. Take the simple loop example presented in the Introduction for the **for** structure and program it using all three structures.

Step 1: Start Your Compiler

Start your compiler if it is not already running.

Step 2: Type In Code for the *for* Structure

Your code should be typed in exactly as follows. Save the program as **Project 5-1A.cpp**. Remember to save your code after typing in the first line or two of your program, and then as often as possible thereafter.

```
// Project 5-1A
// This is the first of three simple loop comparisons
// This project uses the for structure.


#include <iostream.h>

main()
{

    for (int counter = 1; counter <= 10; counter++)
        cout << "This is a for structure.\n";

    return 0;
}
```

Step 3: Save Your Program

Once you have finished typing in your code, save your code one final time before compiling your program.

Step 4: Build, Link, Run

Enter the commands necessary to build, link, and run your program. If errors occur during any of these processes, check your code, correct any errors, and rerun the program.

You should have 10 lines of "This is a for structure." displayed on your screen.

Step 5: Review Your Code

Concentrate on reviewing the lines of code shown below. You should understand the rest of the program.

```
for (int counter = 1; counter <= 10; counter++)
        cout << "This is a for structure.\n";
```

1. Explain what happens when these two lines of code are executed.

_____

_____

_____

_____

_____

2. Explain why the clauses enclosed in the parentheses in the *for* line are separated by semicolons.

_____

3. Explain the significance of using `counter <= 10` vs. using `counter < 11`.

_____

_____

_____

_____

Step 6: Type In Code for the *while* Structure

Now you'll rewrite this sample program using the *while* structure. The only changes will occur in the body of the program. Your code should be typed in exactly as follows. Save the program as **Project 5-1B.cpp**. Remember to save your code after typing in the first line or two of your program, and then as often as possible thereafter.

```
// Project 5-1B
// This is the second of three simple loop comparisons
// This project uses the while structure.


#include <iostream.h>

main()
{
    int counter = 1;

    while ( counter <= 10 ) {
        cout << "This is a while structure.\n";
        counter++;
    }

    return 0;
}
```

Step 7: Save Your Program

Once you have finished typing in your code, save your code one final time before compiling your program.

Step 8: Build, Link, Run

Enter the commands necessary to build, link, and run your program. If errors occur during any of these processes, check your code, correct any errors, and rerun the program.

You should have 10 lines of "This is a while structure." displayed on your screen.

Step 9: Review Your Code

Let's concentrate on reviewing the *while* structure. Take a look at the code shown below.

```
int counter = 1;

while ( counter <= 10 ) {
    cout << "This is a while structure.\n";
    counter++;
}
```

1. Explain why you now have a separate variable initialization statement.

_____

_____

_____

2. Explain the condition in parentheses immediately after the while command.

_____

_____

3. Explain why you use braces around the commands in the body of the while structure.

_____

_____

4. Explain counter++.

_____

_____

5. The counter++ code is an example of ***postincrement***. Explain the difference between ***preincrement*** and postincrement.

_____

_____

_____

Step 10: Type In Code for the *do/while* Structure

Now you'll rewrite this sample program using the *do/while* structure. Again, the only changes will occur in the body of the program. Your code should be typed in exactly as follows. Save this program with the name: **Project 5-1C.cpp**. Remember to save your code after typing in the first line or two of your program, and then as often as possible thereafter.

```
// Project 5-1C
// This is the third of three simple loop comparisons
// This project uses the do/while structure.

#include <iostream.h>

main()
{
    int counter = 1;

    do {
        cout << "This is a do/while structure.\n";
        counter++;
    } while (counter <= 10);

    return 0;
}
```

Step 11: Save Your Program

Once you have finished typing in your code, save your code one final time before compiling your program.

Step 12: Build, Link, Run

Enter the commands necessary to build, link, and run your program. If errors occur during any of these processes, check your code, correct any errors, and rerun the program.

You should have 10 lines of "This is a do/while structure." displayed on your screen.

Step 13: Review Your Code

Concentrate on reviewing the *do/while* structure. Take a look at the code shown below.

```
int counter = 1;

do {
    cout << "This is a do/while structure.\n";
    counter++;
} while (counter <= 10);
```

1. Explain the basic layout difference between the while and the do/while structure.

_____

_____

_____

_____

_____

2. Explain the need for the braces in the do portion of the structure.

_____

3. Explain when the condition is checked in the do/while vs. the while structure.

_____

_____

An alternative to the way you coded the do/while example follows:

```
int counter = 1;

  do {
      cout << "This is a do/while structure.\n";

  } while (++counter <= 10);
```

104

Compare this code to the first do/while example and answer the following questions.

1. Explain the following line of code:

```
}   while (++counter <= 10);
```

_____

_____

2. Explain the difference between ++counter and counter++. Use proper terminology.

_____

_____

3. Give your opinion as to which method you prefer.

_____

_____

You now have a working example of the three repetition structures.

PROJECT 5-2:
Simple Menu with a while Repetition Structure

Ⓑ

Take another look at modifying the simple menu program. You'll remember that you created the simple menu in Project 2-2 and then modified it with an if/else structure in Project 4-1. This time, you'll modify it with a while repetition structure. The while structure will allow you to continually loop through the main menu until you choose to exit. Very few programs force the user to exit after making one choice and then performing one task; they loop back around so that the user may make another choice. That's the functionality you will add in this project.

You also will need to add a clear screen function to make these menu loops work properly. However, clear screen functions are specific to compilers and operating systems. For you to implement the proper clear screen method in your version of these projects, you will need to get the proper coding from your instructor. If you are using the South-Western text, _Introduction To Computer Science Using C++,_ by Todd Knowlton, you can visit the following Web site for clear screen information: _http://www.ProgramCPP.com_ and the topic is _6.2.1._

Step 1: Start Your Compiler

Start your compiler if it is not already running.

Step 2: Modify Your Code

Open the **Project 4-1.cpp** file. Save it as **Project 5-2.cpp**. Modify the code exactly as shown below. Remember to save your code as you modify it.

```
// Project 5-2 (Was Project 4-1)
// Programmer: (Your Name)
// This program will introduce the basics of a while repetition structure

#include <iostream.h>


// The main function

main()
{

// Initialize the menu choice variable

int Choice;

while (1) {


// The following creates a heading for our menu.

    cout << "\t\t\t/////////////////////////////\n";
    cout << "\t\t\t//////// RECORD /////////\n";
    cout << "\t\t\t///////// MENU //////////\n";
    cout << "\t\t\t/////////////////////////////\n";

// The following displays your menu choices on the screen

    cout << "\n\t\t\t1) Add A New Record \n";
    cout << "\t\t\t2) Modify An Existing Record \n";
    cout << "\t\t\t3) Delete An Existing Record \n";
    cout << "\t\t\t4) View/Print An Existing Record \n";
    cout << "\t\t\t5) Exit \n";
    cout << "\n\t\t\tPlease Enter Your Choice:  ";

// The cin command accepts the user's choice

    cin >> Choice;

// The following IF/ELSE structure provides output based on your choice.
// AND it provides quicker execution because of a possible early exit from
// the choices.

    if (Choice == 1)
        cout << "\n\t\t\tYou chose to add a new record.\n\t\t\t";

    else if (Choice == 2)
        cout << "\n\t\t\tYou chose to modify a record.\n\t\t\t";

    else if (Choice == 3)
        cout << "\n\t\t\tYou chose to delete a record.\n\t\t\t";

    else if (Choice == 4)
```

```
          cout << "\n\t\t\tYou chose to view/print a record.\n\t\t\t";

   else if (Choice == 5)
          {
            cout << "\n\t\t\tYou chose to Exit this menu.\n\t\t\t";
            break;
          }
   else
          {
            cout << "\n\t\t\tYour choice is NOT valid!\n";
            cout << "\t\t\tPlease enter a CORRECT choice!\n\n\t\t\t";
          }
   }
// The return statement ends the function.

   return 0;

}
```

Remember to save your code again after typing in the remainder of your program.

Step 3: Build, Link, Run

Enter the commands necessary to build, link, and run your program. If errors occur during any of these processes, check your code, correct any errors, and recompile the program.

Test your program by selecting all the valid choices and by making a few invalid choices. Your menu should execute the way it always has, at least on the surface. Again, remember that without the proper clear screen function the repeated menu will appear part way down the screen.

Step 4: Review Your Code

This while structure is slightly different than the one shown in Project 5-1. Take a look at three specific lines of the while structure.

```
while (1) {
```

1. The keyword while is followed by its condition statement. Explain this specific condition statement.

_____

_____

```
}
```

2. Explain why braces surround the entire if/else selection structure.

_____

_____

3. Explain what the above line of code signifies.

_____

4. Explain why choice 5 in the code below is the only choice to contain a break statement.

```
else if (Choice == 5)
        {
        cout << "\n\t\t\tYou chose to Exit this menu.\n\t\t\t";
        break;
        }
```

_____

_____

_____

5. Now that you've seen this entire program operate, explain the basic operation of the while(1) repetition structure.

_____

P R O J E C T   5 - 3 : Repeating a Screen

Now you are going to put your talent to work! Follow the steps below and the hints provided to complete this project. Also, make sure you make use of the space provided to list the things you do inside each step.

This project is simple. You're going to take your enhanced menu—the menu that uses the switch selection structure to branch to your Data Input Screen. This enhanced menu was completed in Project 5-2.

Step 1: Start Your Compiler

Start your compiler if it is not already running.

Step 2: Open the Project 2-2.cpp File

Open the code file for Project 5-2. _Immediately_ save it as **Project 5-3.cpp**. Then print a hard copy of the code. Or you can work from the code of Project 5-2.cpp below.

```
// Project 5-2 (Was Project 4-1)
// Programmer: (Your Name)
// This program will introduce the basics of a while repetition structure

#include <iostream.h>


// The main function
```

```
main()
{

// Initialize the menu choice variable

int Choice;

while (1) {


// The following creates a heading for our menu.

    cout  << "\t\t\t/////////////////////////////////\n";
    cout  << "\t\t\t///////// RECORD /////////////\n";
    cout  << "\t\t\t/////////  MENU  //////////////\n";
    cout  << "\t\t\t/////////////////////////////////\n";

// The following displays your menu choices on the screen

    cout << "\n\t\t\t1) Add A New Record \n";
    cout << "\t\t\t2) Modify An Existing Record \n";
    cout << "\t\t\t3) Delete An Existing Record \n";
    cout << "\t\t\t4) View/Print An Existing Record \n";
    cout << "\t\t\t5) Exit \n";
    cout << "\n\t\t\tPlease Enter Your Choice:   ";

// The cin command accepts the user's choice

    cin >> Choice;

// The following IF/ELSE structure provides output based on your choice.
// AND it provides quicker execution because of a possible early exit from
// the choices.

    if (Choice == 1)
         cout << "\n\t\t\tYou chose to add a new record.\n\t\t\t";

    else if (Choice == 2)
         cout << "\n\t\t\tYou chose to modify a record.\n\t\t\t";

    else if (Choice == 3)
         cout << "\n\t\t\tYou chose to delete a record.\n\t\t\t";

    else if (Choice == 4)
         cout << "\n\t\t\tYou chose to view/print a record.\n\t\t\t";

    else if (Choice == 5)
         {
           cout << "\n\t\t\tYou chose to Exit this menu.\n\t\t\t";
           break;
         }
    else
```

```
            {
                cout << "\n\t\t\tYour choice is NOT valid!\n";
                cout << "\t\t\tPlease enter a CORRECT choice!\n\n\t\t\t";
            }
    }
// The return statement ends the function.

    return 0;

}
```

Step 3: Modify Your Code

The first thing you are going to do is place the code for the function prototype, the function call, and the function definition in place.

1. Using the code from the *Project 4-3.cpp* file, copy and paste the necessary lines of code into this project. If necessary, write down the lines of code that you need to transfer.

_____

_____

_____

_____

_____

_____

_____

_____

_____

_____

_____

_____

_____

_____

_____

_____

_____

_____

_____

_____

_____

_____

_____

_____

_____

_____

_____

_____

_____

_____

_____

_____

_____

_____

2. Once you have inserted the code, save the file, and then build, link, and run it to make sure that you can get to the Data Input function. This will also help you make sure that your program still executes the way it's supposed to.

3. Now, you should think through the repetition structure for the Data Input screen. You know that if the user selects this choice, he or she will want to enter at least one new record; therefore, you want this function to execute at least once. However, you do not know how many new records the user will need to input, so that means letting the user control the exit. If those are the parameters for the repetition, then what repetition structure do you need to use? Explain why.

_____

_____

_____

_____

_____

4. Now, design the code. You want the loop to begin automatically since you know that at least one record will be entered. After the user enters the first record, you will want to ask if the user wishes to continue. If so, you loop. If not, you break. In the space below, write the code you need for your loop.

_____

_____

_____

_____

_____

_____

_____

_____

_____

_____

5. Type in the repetition structure code you need to make your loop work properly.

Step 4: Build, Link, Run

Once you have your code typed in, save the file. Then, build, link, and run the program. If there are syntax errors, correct them and then resave and recompile. If there are no errors, then you must test every option on each menu to make sure your logic works properly.

Step 5: Testing Your Program

Run your program and test the functioning of each and every choice on both menus. Make sure that each choice executes exactly as it is supposed to execute. *And,* make sure that you do *not* get caught in an endless loop.

 HOT TIP

Before you get caught in an endless loop, make sure you know what your break character is for your operating system. For DOS, it's `<ctrl-c>`. If you are not sure, ask your instructor.

Step 6: Check Your Code

If you are having major problems at this point, check your code against the code shown below.

```
// Project 5-3 (Was Project 5-2)
// Programmer: (Your Name)
// This program will introduce the basics of a while repetition structure
// nested within a while repetition structure.

#include <iostream.h>

// Function prototype for the addition of the Data Input function

void dataInput();

// The main function

main()
{

// Initialize the menu choice variable

int Choice;

while (1) {
```

```
// The following creates a heading for your menu.

    cout << "\t\t\t//////////////////////////////\n";
    cout << "\t\t\t/////////  RECORD  //////////\n";
    cout << "\t\t\t/////////   MENU   //////////\n";
    cout << "\t\t\t//////////////////////////////\n";

// The following displays your menu choices on the screen

    cout << "\n\t\t\t1) Add A New Record \n";
    cout << "\t\t\t2) Modify An Existing Record \n";
    cout << "\t\t\t3) Delete An Existing Record \n";
    cout << "\t\t\t4) View/Print An Existing Record \n";
    cout << "\t\t\t5) Exit \n";
    cout << "\n\t\t\tPlease Enter Your Choice:   ";

// The cin command accepts the user's choice

    cin >> Choice;

// The following IF/ELSE structure provides output based on your choice.
// AND it provides quicker execution because of a possible early exit from
// the choices.

    if (Choice == 1)
         dataInput();

    else if (Choice == 2)
         cout << "\n\t\t\tYou chose to modify a record.\n\t\t\t";

    else if (Choice == 3)
         cout << "\n\t\t\tYou chose to delete a record.\n\t\t\t";

    else if (Choice == 4)
         cout << "\n\t\t\tYou chose to view/print a record.\n\t\t\t";

    else if (Choice == 5)
       {
         cout << "\n\t\t\tYou chose to Exit this menu.\n\t\t\t";
         break;
       }

    else
       {
         cout << "\n\t\t\tYour choice is NOT valid!\n";
         cout << "\t\t\tPlease enter a CORRECT choice!\n\n\t\t\t";
       }
    }
// The return statement ends the function.

    return 0;

}
```

```
// function definition
void dataInput()
{

    // Initialize the necessary variables.

    char fname[20];      // First Name
    char mi[1];          // Middle Initial
    char lname[30];      // Last Name
    char phnum[7];       // Phone Number not including area code
    char dob[10];        // Date of Birth, Format MM/DD/YYYY
    char email[30];      // E-mail address
    int answer = 1;      // User's choice of entering data or not


    // Set up the input screen
    // Create the Heading

    cout << "\t\t\t%%%%%%%%%%%%%%%%%%%%%%%%%%%%%%\n";
    cout << "\t\t\t%%%%%% Contact Name %%%%%%\n";
    cout << "\t\t\t%%%%%%%%%%% and %%%%%%%%%%%\n";
    cout << "\t\t\t%%%%%%%%%% Address %%%%%%%%%\n";
    cout << "\t\t\t%%%%%%%%%%%%%%%%%%%%%%%%%%%%%%\n";

    // Inform the user as to what this screen is to be used for.

    cout << "\n\n\tUse this screen to input a new contact to your Personal
Phone Book.\n";

  while (answer == 1) {

    // Get the user to enter information.

    cout << "\n\nEnter Contact's First Name:\t";
    cin >> fname;

    cout << "\nEnter Contact's Middle Initial:\t";
    cin >> mi;

    cout << "\nEnter Contact's Last Name:\t";
    cin >> lname;

    cout << "\nEnter Contact's Phone Number\n";
    cout << "(without the area code):\t";
    cin >> phnum;

    cout << "\nEnter Contact's Date of Birth:\n";
    cout << "(use MM/DD/YYYY format):\t";
    cin >> dob;

    cout << "\nEnter Contact's E-Mail Address:\t";
    cin >> email;

    cout << "\nWould you like to enter another record?";
```

```
        cout << "\nEnter 1 for Yes, 2 for No:   ";
        cin >> answer;

        if (answer != 1)
                break;

        else
                continue;
}

        // This function does not need to return a value
}
```

If your code differs, but your program works—that's great! Not all programs that work the same are coded the same. With this program, you can actually loop with the Main Menu and the Data Input screen until the user decides to exit.

Step 7: Review Your Code

At this point, discuss your finished program with your teacher and classmates to reinforce your ability to analyze C++ code.

P R O J E C T   5 - 4 : Compound Interest

In previous lessons, you coded programs that deal with computing interest for short periods of time. You even modified these programs to calculate simple interest over a period of years, although interest is normally compounded when someone borrows, or invests, money for more than a year. Now you're going to actually compound interest on your long-term investments the way it's supposed to be done.

Step 1: Start Your Compiler

If your compiler is not already running, start it now.

Step 2: Design Your Program

You know you'll need a main function. You will also need some variables of a type that can be used for math calculations. And, since compounding means to add interest upon interest, the program must contain a repetition structure.

1. In the space below, write the code needed for the main function while leaving space for the additional code you will need. Make sure you include the iostream and the math header files. Whether you use the math header file will depend on the calculation that you use for compounding your interest.

_____

_____

_____

1 1 5

_____

_____

_____

_____

_____

_____

_____

_____

_____

_____

_____

2. Add in the variables you will need for your calculation. You know you'll need a variable for principal, interest rate, and length of time. You can assume that interest will compound monthly. Therefore, if you are borrowing for a period of years, you'll need to convert years into months. And, you will need to convert the annual interest rate into a monthly interest rate. Then, you'll need to convert the interest rate into a decimal. So, you will need at least five variables. Write down the variable names and types that you will be using.

_____

_____

_____

_____

Step 3: Type in Your Code

Type in the code as you've written it so far. Save the program as **Project 5-4.cpp**. _Remember:_ Save often as you type in the code. Add comments to your code as you enter it.

Step 4: Design Your Repetition Structure

You know that you will need to compute interest each and every month for which your money will be invested. Therefore, you know you will have a fixed number of repetitions.

1. Which repetition structure does that suggest? Explain your answer.

_____

_____

You also know that your answer will need to be reused each time you add interest. This may suggest a slightly different assignment operator.

2. Code your repetition structure. Remember to add the additional variable to your variable list and to your code. Design your repetition structure below.

_____

_____

_____

_____

_____

_____

_____

_____

Step 5: Type In Your Code

Type in the additional code that you've written. Remember to save the program often as you type in the code. Add comments to your code as your enter it.

Step 6: Save Your Program

When you have completed typing the code, save your program once more before moving on to the next step.

Step 7: Build, Link, Run

Enter the commands necessary to build, link, and run your program. If errors occur during any of these processes, check your code, correct any errors, and rerun the program.

Remember to save your program any time you make changes!

Test your program by computing the answer to your investment with a calculator. The basic formula for compounded interest is as follows:

Total = principal + (principal x the interest rate per period)

Then move your total amount back into principal and perform the calculation again. The calculation is looped for the total number of months for which you've invested your money.

You now have a program that provides a useful calculation to your users. And it includes a repetition structure. Now they can figure out how much money they will make on their investments!

Step 8: Explain Your Program

If you are having major problems at this point, check your code against the code shown below.

```
// Project 5-4 Compound Interest
// Programmer: <Your Name>
// This program will calculate compound interest on an investment
// using a for repetition structure.

// Include the header file
#include <iostream.h>

// Begin the main function
main()
{
    // Initialize the variables
```

```cpp
    double principal, original;
    double intRate, intPerPeriod;
    double years, periods;

    // Get info from the user
    cout << "Enter the amount of money you want to invest: ";
    cin >> principal;

    cout << "\nEnter the interest rate you will earn: ";
    cin >> intRate;

    cout << "\nEnter the number of years your money will be invested: ";
    cin >> years;

    // Move the principal to another variable for the final cout statement
    original = principal;

    // Change years into months
    periods = years * 12;

    // Change annual interest into decimal and monthly rate
    intPerPeriod = intRate/100/12;

    // Calculate compound interest
    for (int counter = 1; counter <= periods; counter++)
        principal += (principal * intPerPeriod);

    // Tell the user the answer
    cout << "\nYour investment of " << original
        << " will earn you a total of " << principal
        << " in " << years << " years. \n";

    // End the function
    return 0;
}
```

Make sure you keep practicing your ability to analyze and explain C++ code. Explain each line or block of code from your program in the space provided below.

_____
_____
_____
_____
_____
_____
_____
_____
_____
_____
_____
_____

_____

_____

_____

_____

_____

_____

_____

_____

_____

_____

_____

_____

_____

_____

_____

_____

_____

_____

_____

_____

_____

_____

_____

_____

_____

_____

_____

_____

_____

When you're finished, discuss your answers with your teacher and classmates to reinforce your ability to analyze C++ code.

P R O J E C T   5 - 5 : Testing for EOF

The program you will code in this project deals with testing the input for an end of file (EOF) flag. Such a test comes in handy when you are not sure how many items the user needs to input. You handle this by using the **cin.get()** function which tests for an EOF character automatically. If the user inputs the EOF character, then the program ends.

The basic structure of this test is to perform/execute commands until you hit the EOF character. This logic suggests that you do *not* use the for repetition structure since you do *not* know how many times you will need to loop. Therefore, you will use either the do/while or the while repetition structure.

You will enter survey results to be accumulated and then displayed to the screen. The participants in the survey were asked to agree, disagree, or offer no opinion to a question. The question was asked at a local mall to teenagers only. Since you had 24 students asking the question, you don't know how many responses to expect. All you know is that you have a huge pile of papers!

Step 1: Start Your Compiler

If your compiler is not already running, start it now.

Step 2: Design Your Program

> **HOT TIP**
>
> Use the while structure to set up the repetition, then use the switch structure within the while to accumulate the results.

1. In the space below, write the code needed for your program. (*Hint:* Outline your main function, set up the program flow, and create the variables. Prompt users to enter the information you need while making sure that they know about the EOF option with which to end their input. If the user enters an incorrect choice, let him or her know it. Add up the survey results by response. Display the totals of each category on the screen.)

_____

_____

_____

_____

_____

_____

_____

_____

_____

_____

_____

_____

_____

_____

_____

_____

_____

_____

_____

_____

_____

_____

_____

_____

_____

_____

_____

_____

_____

_____

_____

_____

_____

_____

_____

_____

_____

_____

_____

Step 3: Type in Your Program

Type in the code as you create each section. Save the program as **Project 5-5.cpp**. _Remember:_ Save often as you type in the code. Add comments to your code as your enter it.

Step 4: Save Your Program

When you have completed typing the code, save your program once more before moving on to the next step.

Step 5: Build, Link, Run

Enter the commands necessary to build, link, and run your program. If errors occur during any of these processes, check your code, correct any errors, and rerun the program.

Remember to save your program any time you make changes!

When you run your program you will need to test the program for proper execution. This includes input options, switching and accumulating, repetition, and exiting the program.

Step 6: Explain Your Program

Make sure you keep practicing your ability to analyze and explain C++ code. Explain each line or block of code from your program in the space below.

_____

_____

_____

_____

When you're finished, discuss your answers with your teacher and classmates to reinforce your ability to analyze C++ code.

If you are having major problems at this point, check your code against the code shown below.

```cpp
// Project 5-5  EOF Test
// Programmer: <Your Name>
// This program tabulates the results of a student survey.
// It also provides an error message for improper entries.
// Notice the use of the while and the switch structures.

#include <iostream.h>


main()
{
    int response,
        Acount = 0,
        Dcount = 0,
        NOcount = 0;

    cout << "Enter the participant's response.\n";
    cout << "A - Agree, D- Disagree, N- No Opinion\n";
    cout << "Enter the EOF character to end the input.\n";
    cout << "Response: ";

    while ( (response = cin.get()) != EOF)
    {
        switch (response)
        {
            case 'A':
            case 'a':
                ++Acount;
                break;

            case 'D':
            case 'd':
                ++Dcount;
                break;

            case 'N':
            case 'n':
                ++NOcount;
                break;

            default:
                cout <<"\nIncorrect response!" << " Enter A, D, or N" << endl;
                break;
        }
    }

    cout << "\nThe total number of students agreeing is "
         << Acount << ".";

    cout << "\nThe total number of students disagreeing is "
         << Dcount  << ".";
```

1 2 3

```
        cout << "\nThe total number of students with no opinion is "
             << NOcount << "." << endl;

        return 0;
    }
```

Two differences that should be pointed out, again, in this switch selection structure is the cin.get() and the case testing for both upper and lower case. The cin.get() takes the character input from the keyboard and places it in an integer variable. This allows you to read characters as integers. More importantly, it will allow the cin.get() to compare against an end-of-file character for repetition termination.

You now have a program that allows the user to input an unknown amount of information because it tests for EOF. You can use this test with any of the programs that you have developed that allow a variable amount of input. So go forth and integrate control structures where necessary into your code!

Summary

Control structures are a very important part of programming. In this lesson, you concentrated on repetition structures. You looped your Main Menu program, and then added a loop for the Data Input screen using while repetition structures. This created multiple loops running within the same program. Once you add the proper clear screen functions to your programs you will have a menu system that works the way it's supposed to. Users control what functions they want to perform! And they choose when they want to exit the program. Remember, programs do not usually execute one particular function and then quit. They usually provide the user with continual access to multiple activities until the user wants to quit.

You also learned how to design calculations that need to repeat. One of the most obvious and useful calculations is the computation of compound interest. In earlier projects, you created programs that calculated simple interest. Compounding interest is a natural add-on to your collection of calculations! Since you knew, or at least could calculate from user-provided information, how many times the calculation needed to repeat, you used the for repetition structure.

The last project you created tested for an EOF character. Such a structured program allows the user to control the amount of information being input. This project reinforced the cin.get function, as well as the switch selection structure and the while repetition structure.

Now you are capable of creating repetition structures so that you do not need to rerun the same program every time you switch from function to function. You should be getting a pretty good handle on integrated program design!

LESSON 5 REVIEW QUESTIONS

SHORT ANSWER

Define the following in the space provided.

1. while

_____

_____

_____

2. do/while

_____

_____

3. for

_____

_____

4. Repetition control structure

_____

_____

5. Looping

_____

6. do

_____

_____

7. counter

_____

8. Increment

_____

9. Postincrement

_____

10. Preincrement

_____

11. Break

_____

12. while (1)

_____

13. Assignment operator

_____

_____

14. Escape character

_____

15. EOF character

_____

16. Endless loop

_____

17. cin.get()

_____

_____

WRITTEN QUESTIONS

Write your answers to the following questions in the space provided.

1. Why are repetition control structures used?

_____

2. Explain the differences between the while and do/while repetition structures.

_____

_____

_____

_____

3. Explain the appropriate use of the for repetition structure.

_____

_____

4. Explain the difference between preincrement and postincrement.

_____

_____

5. Explain the use of the cin.get() function.

_____

_____

6. Explain the use of the while (1) repetition structure.

_____

_____

7. Explain how the cin.get() allows the user to control variable amounts of input.

_____

_____

_____

8. Explain the use of the counter in the for structure.

_____

_____

9. Explain the syntax of the for structure.

_____

_____

_____

10. Write two lines of code that increment a variable—one line for a preincrement, and one line for a postincrement.

_____

_____

_____

TESTING YOUR SKILLS

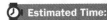

Estimated Time:
Application 5-1A 45 minutes
Application 5-1B 1 $\frac{1}{4}$ hours
Application 5-2   1 $\frac{1}{4}$ hours

APPLICATION 5-1A

Change the repetition structure in Project 5-2 to a do/while structure. Save your modified program as **App5-1A.cpp**.

APPLICATION 5-1B

Change the repetition structure in Project 5-2 to a for structure. This will prove to be more difficult than Application 5-1A. You will need to research empty for statements—**for (;;)**. Save your modified program as **App5-1B.cpp**.

APPLICATION 5-2

Create a program that will average the grades you receive for your assignments during this grading period. Use a while structure that tests for EOF, unless you know the exact number of graded assignments that you will have this grading period. In that case, a for structure might work better.

While you're at it, add a selection structure that will take your average and assign a letter grade to it based on your school's grading system. Save this program as **App5-2.cpp**.

CRITICAL THINKING Ⓐ

SCANS

Take the group of calculation programs/functions that you created in the Critical Thinking section of Lesson 3 and the menu overlay you created in the Critical Thinking section of Lesson 4. Add repetition structures to your menu and your selections off the menu so that the user can perform multiple calculations without exiting and rerunning the program.

When you finish this assignment, you will have a complete multiple-selection, repetitive program to call your own!

MULTIPLE FUNCTIONS

OBJECTIVES

Upon completion of this lesson, you should be able to:

■ Organize a program into logical functions.

■ Design function structures.

■ Formulate code for each function.

■ Create a header file for function prototypes.

■ Design a user interface.

■ Implement repetition and selection control structures into your program.

■ Assemble program components into a cohesive unit.

⏱ Estimated Time: 8 hours

Introduction

This lesson pulls together everything you've done in Lessons 1-5, and illustrates the use and benefit of multiple functions. You will learn how to separate a program into functions that can be reused, or "called" over and over again.

The benefit to your program code is that the main function shrinks! The "heavy-duty" part of the code is stored in the function prototypes and the definitions, enabling the main function to simply use what it needs when it needs it. The ease of this will become evident as you work your way through this lesson.

This lesson will focus on the following:

■ **Designing a program structure and formulating code for the structure.** You will create a program structure that will perform multiple functions. You will be responsible for using the skills you've acquired so far to design and code the entire program.

■ **Evaluating the program for correctness.** Before dividing the program into functions you'll want to make sure that it functions properly. That way you have a working program with which to compare your changes.

■ **Organizing the program into logical functions, designing the function structures, and formulating code for each function.** Once you have the program working, you will take a look at which functions "belong" together. You will find some choices and calculations that will be able to

129

function as standalone programs. That is one way to look at separating a large program into smaller components. Once you know how to split the program into "pieces," you'll be able to design and code each individual function. Remember that you'll be creating function prototypes, function calls, and function descriptions.

■ **Creating a header file for function prototypes.** Creating a header file for the prototypes used in your program is an easy way to remember to include them.

■ **Designing a user interface.** It must be easy for users to interact with your programs. The easier it is for users to get their work done, the better it will be for the programmer!

■ **Implementing repetition and selection control structures into a program.** Programs usually do not perform one task and then exit. They allow the user to control choices and then exit when they are finished. You will make sure your programs execute in the appropriate manner.

■ **Assembling program components into a cohesive unit.** You will begin by creating a cohesive program and then breaking it into smaller and more manageable functions. By keeping track of changes, and by continually testing the program's execution, you will be able to solve any integration problems as they happen.

So, get ready to integrate!

PROJECT 6 - 1 A : The Payroll Program

In this project, you're going to design and code a payroll calculation program. This program will form the basis for subsequent projects in this lesson.

Payroll is a standard and necessary business function. Anyone employed by a company wants to get paid. The company has to earn money from which it can pay employees, and it has to calculate how much each employee should get paid.

Payroll is computed on a regular cycle: weekly, bi-weekly, semi-monthly, or monthly.

Step 1: Start Your Compiler

Start your compiler if it is not already running.

Step 2: Design the Program Structure

Before you begin to design your program structure, you need to understand what it is that you're trying to accomplish. If you have ever been employed, you probably have a general understanding of how payroll works. However, to design a payroll program, you have to know details, details, and more details. So, the first thing you will do is diagram the actual payroll process.

1. Diagram your understanding of the payroll process. You can use a flowchart, pseudocode, or a narrative—anything that makes sense to you.

_____

_____

_____

_____

_____

130

_____

_____

_____

_____

_____

_____

_____

_____

_____

_____

_____

_____

_____

_____

_____

_____

_____

_____

_____

_____

_____

_____

_____

_____

2. Now compare your diagram to the following narrative, which is a close representation of the payroll process.

The first thing you need to do is to figure out the payroll cycle. Assume you will pay everyone on a weekly basis. Then you need to know when the workweek starts and ends. You will run from Sunday through Saturday. You then need to calculate the total hours each employee works during the workweek. A payroll clerk will enter hours for each employee on a day-by-day basis. Employees are all hourly. In an actual company, some employees would be salaried and some paid on commission.

Once you know the total hours worked by an employee, you will then need to differentiate between regular and overtime hours. Regular hours are paid at the normal hourly rate, whereas any hours over the first 40 hours worked are paid at 1-1/2 times the normal hourly rate.

131

Now that you know the total hours, regular hours, and overtime hours (if any), you can calculate gross pay. Gross pay is the total of the following calculations:

regular hours x *regular pay rate* = *regular pay*

overtime hours x *regular pay rate* x 1.5 = *overtime pay*

regular pay + *overtime pay* = *gross pay*

Once you know gross pay you can calculate the amount of taxes that need to be withheld from the employee's pay. These tax deductions are required by law and must be accurate. Payroll tax laws vary from state to state, which is one reason that there are companies in existence that do nothing but run payroll for other companies. Payroll tax calculations can be very complex, but simplified calculations will be used for your program.

Federal income tax withholding is dependent on annual income, marital status, number of dependents, pay period, and any additional voluntary withholding. As you can probably guess, this tax calculation is complex. You will simplify it by choosing between two marital status choices (married or single). Married employees pay 15 percent federal income tax, and single employees pay 20 percent.

The other tax deductions—Social Security, state income taxes, and local income taxes—are usually a percentage of your entire pay. However, Social Security withholding does have a salary cap. Once you hit the salary cap, no more Social Security is deducted from your pay *for that year.*

You will use the Married/Single choice to determine the federal tax percent, and straight percentages for each of the other payroll taxes. You will also ignore the Social Security salary cap. It's your job to find out the correct tax rates for your state!

In order to calculate payroll deductions, you simply multiply gross pay by each tax percentage. The answer is the amount of tax to be deducted for that government entity. But you do need to keep track of the amount of *each* tax deduction. This will have an impact on the number of variables you will need.

At an actual company, you would then test for voluntary deductions—retirement, medical insurance, life insurance, etc. If the employee had signed up for any of these, then you would deduct either a fixed amount or a percentage of gross pay. You will include medical insurance deduction of $10 per pay for single employees and $18 per pay for married employees.

The last thing you need to calculate is net pay. This is how much the employee actually takes home. Net pay is simply gross pay minus all the deductions.

But there is one very important last step—printing the paycheck. In this program you will simply display a payroll report to the screen.

And there you have it—the payroll process in a nutshell! Now, move into coding your program.

Step 3: Create the Code for Your Program Structure

Now that you understand the payroll calculation, begin to code the actual program.

1. In the space below, write the code for the Main function.

_____

_____

_____

_____

_____

2. Split the entire payroll calculation into separate sections. For example, entering and totaling hours; calculating regular, overtime, and total pay; calculating taxes and deductions; and displaying the "pay stub" to the screen.

_____

_____

_____

_____

_____

3. Pseudocode each section and then compare it to the overall pseudocode above.

_____

_____

_____

_____

_____

_____

_____

_____

_____

_____

_____

_____

_____

_____

_____

_____

_____

_____

_____

_____

_____

4. Make a list of all the variables you will need for each section and their type.

_____

_____

_____

_____

_____

_____

_____

_____

_____

_____

5. Code the payroll calculation from the top down. This is a good opportunity to apply the sequence control structure built into C++ compilers.

_____

_____

_____

_____

_____

_____

_____

_____

_____

_____

_____

_____

_____

_____

_____

_____

_____

_____

_____

_____

_____

_____

_____

_____

_____

_____

_____

_____

_____

_____

_____

_____

_____

_____

_____

_____

_____

_____

Step 4: Type in Your Code

Your code should be typed in exactly as you write it. Save this program as **Project 6-1A.cpp**. Remember to save your code after typing in the first line or two of your program, and then as often as possible thereafter.

Step 5: Save Your Program

Once you have finished typing in your code, save your code one final time before compiling your program.

Step 6: Build, Link, Run

Enter the commands necessary to build, link, and run your program. If errors occur during any of these processes, check your code, correct any errors, and rerun the program.

Test your program to see if it calculates properly. Compare it to a few manual calculations.

Step 7: Review Your Code

If the coding becomes difficult, or you simply want something to which to compare your code, review the code below. If your code is different, that's fine. Not everyone programs the same!

```cpp
// Project 6-1A  Huge Payroll Calculation

#include <iostream.h>


main()
{

    // Define the variables & constants
    unsigned int sunHrs = 0, monHrs = 0, tueHrs = 0, wedHrs = 0;
    unsigned int thuHrs = 0, friHrs = 0, satHrs = 0;
    unsigned int regHrs = 0, otHrs = 0, totHrs = 0;
    double hrlyRate, regPay, otPay, grossPay, netPay;
    double fitAmt, ficaAmt, stateAmt, localAmt, totDed;
    int mStatus;
    double medIns = 0;
    double fitWH = 0;
    const double    ficaWH = .0765,
                stateWH = .02,
                localWH = .01;

    // Begin getting info from user
    cout << "Enter hours worked for each day.\n";
    cout << "Enter 0 if no hours worked.\n";

    cout << "\nSunday Hours: ";
    cin >> sunHrs;
    totHrs = sunHrs;

    cout << "\nMonday hours: ";
    cin >> monHrs;
    totHrs += monHrs;

    cout << "\nTuesday Hours: ";
    cin >> tueHrs;
    totHrs += tueHrs;

    cout << "\nWednesday hours: ";
    cin >> wedHrs;
    totHrs += wedHrs;

    cout << "\nThursday Hours: ";
    cin >> thuHrs;
    totHrs += thuHrs;

    cout << "\nFriday hours: ";
    cin >> friHrs;
    totHrs += friHrs;

    cout << "\nSaturday hours: ";
    cin >> satHrs;
    totHrs += satHrs;
```

```
//Separate the hours into regular and overtime
if (totHrs <= 40)
     regHrs = totHrs;
else {
     regHrs = 40;
     otHrs = totHrs - 40;
}


// Calculate gross pay
cout << "\nEnter the employee's pay rate: ";
cin >> hrlyRate;

regPay = regHrs * hrlyRate;
otPay = otHrs * hrlyRate * 1.5;
grossPay = regPay + otPay;


// Calculate taxes section
cout << "\nIs the employee Single or Married?";
cout << "\n (Enter 1 for Single, 2 for Married): ";

cin >> mStatus;


// Decide on  FIT percent based on marital status
if (mStatus == 1)
     fitWH = .20;
else if (mStatus == 2)
     fitWH = .15;
else
     {
         fitWH = 0;
         cout << "\nFIT Error";
     }


// Calculate taxes
fitAmt = grossPay * fitWH;
ficaAmt = grossPay * ficaWH;
stateAmt = grossPay * stateWH;
localAmt = grossPay * localWH;

// Calculate medical insurance
if (mStatus == 1)
     medIns = 10.00;
else if (mStatus == 2)
     medIns = 18.00;
else
     {
         medIns = 0;
         cout << "\nMedical Insurance Error";
     }
```

```cpp
    // Total the deductions
    totDed = fitAmt + ficaAmt + stateAmt + localAmt + medIns;

    // Calculate net pay
    netPay = grossPay - totDed;

    // Print out the payroll information to the screen
    cout << "\nReg. Hrs.\t\tOT Hrs.\t\tPay Rate\t\tGrossPay";
    cout << "\n========\t\t=======\t\t=======\t\t========";
    cout << "\n\t" << regHrs << "\t\t"  << otHrs << "\t\t" << hrlyRate <<
"\t\t\t" << grossPay << endl;

    cout << "\nFIT WH\t\tFICA WH\t\tState WH";
    cout << "\n======\t\t=======\t\t========";
    cout << "\n" << fitAmt << "\t\t" << ficaAmt << "\t\t" << stateAmt << endl;
    cout << "\nLocal WH\tMed. Ins.\tTotal Ded.";
    cout << "\n========\t=========\t==========";
    cout << "\n" << localAmt << "\t\t" << medIns << "\t\t" << totDed << endl;

    cout << "\nNet Pay";
    cout << "\n=======";
    cout << "\n" << netPay << "\n\n";

    // End the main function
    return 0;
}
```

Step 8: Explain Your Code

In the space below, explain the blocks of code you keyed. Explain any special features you may have used in a specific block. If everything in the block is pretty much standard, then the comments should provide adequate explanation.

If you had trouble writing your own code and needed to use the code shown in step 7 above, then write an explanation about that code. Again, you should break the code into manageable blocks in your explanation.

_____

_____

_____

_____

_____

_____

_____

_____

_____

_____

_____

_____

_____

_____

_____

_____

_____

_____

_____

_____

_____

_____

_____

_____

_____

_____

_____

_____

_____

_____

_____

_____

At this point you should have a working payroll program AND you should understand it! This will be very important in the next project.

PROJECT 6-1B : The Hours Entry Function

If your program does more than one thing, or the code cannot be seen without scrolling, then you should be able to separate the program into functions. You can think of each function as a "theme." It focuses on one thing.

The first thing you will do in this project is analyze your payroll program to determine how to separate it into functions.

Step 1: Start Your Compiler

Start your compiler if it is not already running.

Step 2: Print Your Code

Open the **Project 6-1A.cpp** file, and save it as **Project 6-1B.cpp**. Print a copy of the code.

Step 3: Analyze Your Code

You should be looking for logical separations where you can create functions. Look for sections of code that do *one* thing, or better yet, have one theme. For example, the first operation in the program is to input hours. The hours entry operation for all seven days can become a separate function.

1. Review your code for logical separations. In the space below, list the functions you need to create and name each function.

   _____

   _____

   _____

   _____

   _____

   _____

   _____

2. Now that you have a list of functions, determine which functions will be void and which will return a value. Write *void* or *value* next to each function in the list above.

3. For each function, determine the type of value that will be returned and what the value will be. Write the type of value and the value next to the function in the list above.

4. For each function in the list, determine the number, type, and name of the parameters needed by the function. Write them next to the function in the list above.

5. In the space below, write the function prototypes.

   _____

   _____

   _____

   _____

   _____

   _____

   _____

   _____

6. Save all of your function prototypes in a header file named **Lesson6.h**.

Take a look at a function created for the entry of hours.

Step 4: The hoursEntry Function

The entry of hours that each employee worked during the week is the first logical theme. You will ignore the separation of total hours into regular and overtime hours at this point. You know the lines of code that will become the body of the function, so let's create our first function.

1. One method of creating the function properly is to open a brand new text file so that you can copy and paste the necessary code from your main program into a "work file." Then you can copy and paste the function back into your main program after you delete the original sections of code from the main program. Open a new text file. It's not necessary to save it unless you won't finish before the end of class.

2. Copy and paste the lines of code from your main program that make up the hours entry section. Leave the regular and overtime hours calculation where it is. Your work file should look similar to the following.

```cpp
// Begin getting info from user
cout << "Enter hours worked for each day.\n";
cout << "Enter 0 if no hours worked.\n";

cout << "\nSunday Hours: ";
cin >> sunHrs;
totHrs = sunHrs;

cout << "\nMonday hours: ";
cin >> monHrs;
totHrs += monHrs;

cout << "\nTuesday Hours: ";
cin >> tueHrs;
totHrs += tueHrs;

cout << "\nWednesday hours: ";
cin >> wedHrs;
totHrs += wedHrs;

cout << "\nThursday Hours: ";
cin >> thuHrs;
totHrs += thuHrs;

cout << "\nFriday hours: ";
cin >> friHrs;
totHrs += friHrs;

cout << "\nSaturday hours: ";
cin >> satHrs;
totHrs += satHrs;
```

3. You should already have a name for this function, and know its type, the value it will return, and the parameters that will need to be passed to it. For this discussion, the name of this function will be hoursEntry, the function will return total hours, which is an unsigned integer, and since everything is done within the function, nothing needs to be passed to the function.

4. Now put the necessary information into the code. Once you place the function type and name, make sure you place the braces around the body of the function. Remember to place your return statement at the end of the body. When you're done with those three things, the function should look like this:

```cpp
unsigned int hoursEntry()
{

// Begin getting info from user
    cout << "Enter hours worked for each day.\n";
    cout << "Enter 0 if no hours worked.\n";

    cout << "\nSunday Hours: ";
    cin >> sunHrs;
    totHrs = sunHrs;

    cout << "\nMonday hours: ";
    cin >> monHrs;
    totHrs += monHrs;

    cout << "\nTuesday Hours: ";
    cin >> tueHrs;
    totHrs += tueHrs;

    cout << "\nWednesday hours: ";
    cin >> wedHrs;
    totHrs += wedHrs;

    cout << "\nThursday Hours: ";
    cin >> thuHrs;
    totHrs += thuHrs;

    cout << "\nFriday hours: ";
    cin >> friHrs;
    totHrs += friHrs;

    cout << "\nSaturday hours: ";
    cin >> satHrs;
    totHrs += satHrs;


    return totHrs;
}
```

5. Copy your function prototype into your header file, **Lesson6.h**. Make sure you end it with a semicolon in the header file. If you completed this in Step 3, there's no need to repeat it.

6. The next step is to move the variables you need into this function. You can see from the code that you need the variables for each day and total hours. However, instead of moving totHrs into the function, you will create a new variable named tHrs. The reason is that you will be returning total hours as the value to a totHrs variable in the main function. Even though you could use the same name for both variables without them interfering with each other, it makes better practice to use different, but similar names for variables within functions. This will make more sense when you begin passing parameters into functions. The function with variables should look similar to the following.

```
unsigned int hoursEntry()
{
    unsigned int sunHrs = 0, monHrs = 0, tueHrs = 0, wedHrs = 0;
    unsigned int thuHrs = 0, friHrs = 0, satHrs = 0;
    unsigned int tHrs = 0;

// Begin getting info from user
    cout << "Enter hours worked for each day.\n";
    cout << "Enter 0 if no hours worked.\n";

    cout << "\nSunday Hours: ";
    cin >> sunHrs;
    tHrs = sunHrs;

    cout << "\nMonday hours: ";
    cin >> monHrs;
    tHrs += monHrs;

    cout << "\nTuesday Hours: ";
    cin >> tueHrs;
    tHrs += tueHrs;

    cout << "\nWednesday hours: ";
    cin >> wedHrs;
    tHrs += wedHrs;

    cout << "\nThursday Hours: ";
    cin >> thuHrs;
    tHrs += thuHrs;

    cout << "\nFriday hours: ";
    cin >> friHrs;
    tHrs += friHrs;

    cout << "\nSaturday hours: ";
    cin >> satHrs;
    tHrs += satHrs;

    return tHrs;
}
```

Now, you have the function prototype in the header file, and you have the function description complete in the work file. All you need to do is to remove the original sections of code and copy and paste the definition back in. And, don't forget the function call!

7. Delete the original code from your Project 6-1B file. This includes the variables that are now in the hoursEntry function. Make sure you leave the totHrs variable alone! The totHrs variable will remain part of the main function. Copy and paste the hoursEntry function into your main program after the main function ending brace. Leave two or three lines of space between the ending brace and your hoursEntry function definition.

8. Now, add the last few items. First, include your Lesson6.h header file. Second, insert your function call in the appropriate place. Remember, your function returns total hours, so assign that value to the totHrs variable with the function call. Your modified program should look like this:

```cpp
// Project 6-1B  Payroll Calculation with functions

#include <iostream.h>
#include <Lesson6.h>

main()
{

    // Define the variables & constants
    unsigned int regHrs = 0, otHrs = 0, totHrs =0;
    double hrlyRate, regPay, otPay, grossPay, netPay;
    double fitAmt, ficaAmt, stateAmt, localAmt, totDed;
    int mStatus;
    double medIns = 0;
    double fitWH = 0;
    const double   ficaWH = .0765,
                   stateWH = .02,
                   localWH = .01;

    // Get hours from the user
    totHrs = hoursEntry();

    //Separate the hours into regular and overtime
    if (totHrs <= 40)
        regHrs = totHrs;
    else {
        regHrs = 40;
        otHrs = totHrs - 40;
    }


    // Calculate gross pay
    cout << "\nEnter the employee's pay rate: ";
    cin >> hrlyRate;

    regPay = regHrs * hrlyRate;
    otPay = otHrs * hrlyRate * 1.5;
    grossPay = regPay + otPay;


    // Calculate taxes section
    cout << "\nIs the employee Single or Married?";
    cout << "\n (Enter 1 for Single, 2 for Married): ";
```

```
        cin >> mStatus;


    // Decide on  FIT percent based on marital status
    if (mStatus == 1)
        fitWH = .20;
    else if (mStatus == 2)
        fitWH = .15;
    else
        {
            fitWH = 0;
            cout << "\nFIT Error";
        }


    // Calculate taxes
    fitAmt = grossPay * fitWH;
    ficaAmt = grossPay * ficaWH;
    stateAmt = grossPay * stateWH;
    localAmt = grossPay * localWH;

    // Calculate medical insurance
    if (mStatus == 1)
        medIns = 10.00;
    else if (mStatus == 2)
        medIns = 18.00;
    else
        {
            medIns = 0;
            cout << "\nMedical Insurance Error";
        }

    // Total the deductions
    totDed = fitAmt + ficaAmt + stateAmt + localAmt + medIns;

    // Calculate net pay
    netPay = grossPay - totDed;

    // Print out the payroll information to the screen
    cout << "\nReg. Hrs.\t\tOT Hrs.\t\tPay Rate\t\tGrossPay";
    cout << "\n=========\t\t=======\t\t========\t\t========";
    cout << "\n\t" << regHrs << "\t\t"  << otHrs << "\t\t" << hrlyRate <<
"\t\t\t" << grossPay << endl;

    cout << "\nFIT WH\t\tFICA WH\t\tState WH";
    cout << "\n======\t\t=======\t\t========";
    cout << "\n" << fitAmt << "\t\t" << ficaAmt << "\t\t" << stateAmt << endl;
    cout << "\nLocal WH\tMed. Ins.\tTotal Ded.";
    cout << "\n========\t=========\t==========";
    cout << "\n" << localAmt << "\t\t" << medIns << "\t\t" << totDed << endl;

    cout << "\nNet Pay";
```

1 4 5

```cpp
        cout << "\n=======";
        cout << "\n" << netPay << "\n\n";

        // End the main function
        return 0;
}


unsigned int hoursEntry()
{

        unsigned int sunHrs = 0, monHrs = 0, tueHrs = 0, wedHrs = 0;
        unsigned int thuHrs = 0, friHrs = 0, satHrs = 0;
        unsigned int tHrs = 0;

        // Begin getting info from user
        cout << "Enter hours worked for each day.\n";
        cout << "Enter 0 if no hours worked.\n";

        cout << "\nSunday Hours: ";
        cin >> sunHrs;
        tHrs = sunHrs;

        cout << "\nMonday hours: ";
        cin >> monHrs;
        tHrs += monHrs;

        cout << "\nTuesday Hours: ";
        cin >> tueHrs;
        tHrs += tueHrs;

        cout << "\nWednesday hours: ";
        cin >> wedHrs;
        tHrs += wedHrs;

        cout << "\nThursday Hours: ";
        cin >> thuHrs;
        tHrs += thuHrs;

        cout << "\nFriday hours: ";
        cin >> friHrs;
        tHrs += friHrs;

        cout << "\nSaturday hours: ";
        cin >> satHrs;
        tHrs += satHrs;

        return tHrs;
}
```

Step 5: Save Your Program

Once you have finished typing in your code, save your code one final time before compiling your program.

Step 6: Build, Link, Run

Enter the commands necessary to build, link, and run your program. If errors occur during any of these processes, check your code, correct any errors, and rerun the program.

Test your program to see if it executes just like it did before you created the hoursEntry function. Your program should not execute any differently! Functions make programs more organized, easier to debug, and easier to modify. They typically do not change the execution unless other features are added.

You now have one function completed!

PROJECT 6-1C : Two More Functions ①

You will create two more functions in this project.

Step 1: Start Your Compiler

Start your compiler if it is not already running.

Step 2: Open the Project 6-1B.cpp File

Open the code file for **Project 6-1B**. Save the file as **Project 6-1C.cpp**.

Step 3: Create and Enter Federal Withholding and Medical Insurance Functions

Create a function that takes the employee's marital status and returns a federal tax withholding percentage, and create a second function for the medical insurance deduction dollar amount. You need to create the code for the function prototype, the function call and the function definition, although you may already have part of this from Step 3 in Project 6-1B. Once you create the first function, the second is just a copy with a slight modification.

1. Open a new text file so that you can copy and paste the necessary code from your main program into a work file. Then you can copy and paste the functions back into your main program after you delete the original sections of code from the main program. It's not necessary to save the text file unless you won't finish before the end of class.

2. Copy and paste the lines of code from your main program that make up both the "calculate FIT percent" and "medical insurance calculation" sections into your work file.

3. You should already have a name for both functions, know their type, the value each will return, and the parameter that will need to be passed to each. For our discussion, the name of these functions will be FIT and MED, the function will return a percent for one and a dollar amount for the other, which are both doubles, and they both need the same parameter to be passed to the function.

4. Now put the necessary information into your code. Once you place the function type and name, make sure you place the braces around the body of the function. Remember to place your return statement at the end of the body.

5. Copy the function prototype into your header file, **Lesson6.H**. Make sure you end it with a semicolon in the header file. If you completed this in Step 3, there's no need to repeat it.

6. Define the variables you need in each function. You will be using mStatus in both functions and you will need to return values to place in fitWH and medIns. Even though you could use the same name for all three variables without them interfering with each other, it makes better practice to use different, but similar names for variables within functions. This will make more sense when you begin passing parameters into functions. Therefore, choose similar names for these three variables to be used within the functions.

You're almost finished with these functions! You have the function prototypes in the header file, and you have the function descriptions complete in the work file. All you need to do is remove the original sections of code and copy and paste the definition back in! Don't forget the function call.

7. Delete the original code from your Project 6-1C file. Copy and paste both functions into your main program after the main function ending brace. Leave two or three lines of space between the ending brace and your function definitions.

8. Now insert your function calls in the appropriate place. Remember, your one function returns a FIT percentage and the other a medical insurance dollar amount, so assign these values to the proper variable with the function call. Your modified program should look like that shown in Step 5.

Step 4: Build, Link, Run

Once you have your code typed in, save your file. Then build, link, and run your program. If there are syntax errors correct them, and then resave and recompile. If there are no errors, then make sure your payroll program executes just as it did before the addition of the two functions.

Step 5: Check Your Code

If you are having major problems at this point, check your code against the code shown below.

```
// Project 6-1C  Payroll Calculation with functions

#include <iostream.h>
#include <Lesson6.h>

main()
{

    // Define the variables & constants
    unsigned int regHrs = 0, otHrs = 0, totHrs =0;
    double hrlyRate, regPay, otPay, grossPay, netPay;
    double fitAmt, ficaAmt, stateAmt, localAmt, totDed;
    int mStatus;
    double medIns = 0;
    double fitWH = 0;
    const double    ficaWH = .0765,
                    stateWH = .02,
                    localWH = .01;
```

```
    // Get hours from the user
    totHrs = hoursEntry();

    //Separate the hours into regular and overtime
    if (totHrs <= 40)
        regHrs = totHrs;
    else {
        regHrs = 40;
        otHrs = totHrs - 40;
    }


    // Calculate gross pay
    cout << "\nEnter the employee's pay rate: ";
    cin >> hrlyRate;

    regPay = regHrs * hrlyRate;
    otPay = otHrs * hrlyRate * 1.5;
    grossPay = regPay + otPay;


    // Calculate taxes section
    cout << "\nIs the employee Single or Married?";
    cout << "\n (Enter 1 for Single, 2 for Married): ";

    cin >> mStatus;

    // Decide on  FIT percent and Med Ins deduction amount
    // based on marital status
    fitWH = FIT(mStatus);
    medIns = MED(mStatus);

    // Calculate taxes
    fitAmt = grossPay * fitWH;
    ficaAmt = grossPay * ficaWH;
    stateAmt = grossPay * stateWH;
    localAmt = grossPay * localWH;

    // Total the deductions
    totDed = fitAmt + ficaAmt + stateAmt + localAmt + medIns;

    // Calculate net pay
    netPay = grossPay - totDed;

    // Print out the payroll information to the screen
    cout << "\nReg. Hrs.\t\tOT Hrs.\t\tPay Rate\t\tGrossPay";
    cout << "\n=========\t\t=======\t\t========\t\t========";
    cout << "\n\t" << regHrs << "\t\t"  << otHrs << "\t\t" << hrlyRate <<
"\t\t\t" << grossPay << endl;

    cout << "\nFIT WH\t\tFICA WH\t\tState WH";
    cout << "\n======\t\t=======\t\t========";
```

149

```cpp
    cout << "\n" << fitAmt << "\t\t" << ficaAmt << "\t\t" << stateAmt << endl;
    cout << "\nLocal WH\tMed. Ins.\tTotal Ded.";
    cout << "\n========\t=========\t==========";
    cout << "\n" << localAmt << "\t\t" << medIns << "\t\t" << totDed << endl;

    cout << "\nNet Pay";
    cout << "\n=======";
    cout << "\n" << netPay << "\n\n";

    // End the main function
    return 0;
}


unsigned int hoursEntry()
{

    unsigned int sunHrs = 0, monHrs = 0, tueHrs = 0, wedHrs = 0;
    unsigned int thuHrs = 0, friHrs = 0, satHrs = 0;
    unsigned int tHrs = 0;

    // Begin getting info from user
    cout << "Enter hours worked for each day.\n";
    cout << "Enter 0 if no hours worked.\n";

    cout << "\nSunday Hours: ";
    cin >> sunHrs;
    tHrs = sunHrs;

    cout << "\nMonday hours: ";
    cin >> monHrs;
    tHrs += monHrs;

    cout << "\nTuesday Hours: ";
    cin >> tueHrs;
    tHrs += tueHrs;

    cout << "\nWednesday hours: ";
    cin >> wedHrs;
    tHrs += wedHrs;

    cout << "\nThursday Hours: ";
    cin >> thuHrs;
    tHrs += thuHrs;

    cout << "\nFriday hours: ";
    cin >> friHrs;
    tHrs += friHrs;

    cout << "\nSaturday hours: ";
    cin >> satHrs;
```

```
        tHrs += satHrs;

        return tHrs;
}


double FIT(int mStat)
{
    double fWH;

    // Decide on  FIT percent based on marital status
    if (mStat == 1)
            fWH = .20;
    else if (mStat == 2)
            fWH = .15;
    else
        {
            fWH = 0;
            cout << "\nFIT Error";
        }

    return fWH;
}


double MED(int mStat)
{
    double mIns;

    // Calculate medical insurance
    if (mStat == 1)
            mIns = 10.00;
    else if (mStat == 2)
            mIns = 18.00;
    else
        {
            mIns = 0;
            cout << "\nMedical Insurance Error";
        }
    return mIns;
}
```

If your code differs, but your program works—that's great! Not all programs that work the same are coded the same. Now you have a working program that is becoming more organized due to the use of functions.

Step 6: Review Your Code

Discuss your functions, and your program overall, with your teacher and classmates to reinforce your ability to analyze C++ code.

PROJECT 6-1D:
Loop for Additional Employees

The payroll program you've developed so far calculates the payroll amount for one employee and then quits. Payroll programs need to repeat until there are no more employees left to calculate payroll for. At this point you are going to code in the lines needed to make your payroll program loop until the payroll clerk decides there are no employees left.

Step 1: Start Your Compiler

If your compiler is not already running, start it now.

Step 2: Design Your Loop

1. Write down the code needed for your loop. (*Hint:* You will use the while or do/while structure to set up the repetition.)

_____

_____

_____

_____

_____

_____

_____

_____

Step 3: Type in Your Program

Type in the code for your loop. Save the program as **Project 6-1D.cpp**.

Step 4: Build, Link, Run

Enter the commands necessary to build, link, and run your program. If errors occur during any of these processes, check your code, correct any errors, and rerun the program.

Remember to save your program any time you make changes!

When you run your program you will need to test the program for proper execution. This test should prove to be simple. The program simply needs to repeat until the user decides there are no more employees to enter.

Step 5: Explain Your Loop

Make sure you keep practicing your ability to analyze and explain C++ code.

1. Write down the lines you inserted for your loop. There's no need to write all the other commands, simply the lines that pertain directly to your loop.

_____

_____

_____

_____

_____

_____

_____

_____

2. Write down any additional variables you added for your loop.

_____

_____

_____

3. Explain the execution of your loop and the need for the additional variables (if any).

_____

_____

_____

_____

_____

_____

_____

_____

_____

_____

When you're finished, discuss your analysis with your teacher and classmates to reinforce your ability to analyze C++ code.

If you are having major problems at this point, check your code against the code shown below.

```cpp
// Project 6-1D  Payroll Calculation with functions

#include <iostream.h>
#include <Lesson6.h>

main()
{

    // Define the variables & constants
    unsigned int regHrs = 0, otHrs = 0, totHrs =0;
    double hrlyRate, regPay, otPay, grossPay, netPay;
    double fitAmt, ficaAmt, stateAmt, localAmt, totDed;
    int mStatus;
    double medIns = 0;
    double fitWH = 0;
```

153

```
          const double      ficaWH = .0765,
                            stateWH = .02,
                            localWH = .01;
          int answer = 1;

// This creates a loop for the entry of multiple records
while (answer == 1) {


      // Get hours from the user
      totHrs = hoursEntry();

      //Separate the hours into regular and overtime
      if (totHrs <= 40)
            regHrs = totHrs;
      else {
            regHrs = 40;
            otHrs = totHrs - 40;
      }



      // Calculate gross pay
      cout << "\nEnter the employee's pay rate: ";
      cin >> hrlyRate;

      regPay = regHrs * hrlyRate;
      otPay = otHrs * hrlyRate * 1.5;
      grossPay = regPay + otPay;



      // Calculate taxes section
      cout << "\nIs the employee Single or Married?";
      cout << "\n (Enter 1 for Single, 2 for Married): ";

      cin >> mStatus;

      // Decide on  FIT percent and Med Ins deduction amount
      // based on marital status
      fitWH = FIT(mStatus);
      medIns = MED(mStatus);

      // Calculate taxes
      fitAmt = grossPay * fitWH;
      ficaAmt = grossPay * ficaWH;
      stateAmt = grossPay * stateWH;
      localAmt = grossPay * localWH;

      // Total the deductions
      totDed = fitAmt + ficaAmt + stateAmt + localAmt + medIns;

      // Calculate net pay
      netPay = grossPay - totDed;

      // Print out the payroll information to the screen
```

```
        cout << "\nReg. Hrs.\t\tOT Hrs.\t\tPay Rate\t\tGrossPay";
        cout << "\n=========\t\t=======\t\t========\t\t========";
        cout << "\n\t" << regHrs << "\t\t"  << otHrs << "\t\t" << hrlyRate <<
"\t\t\t" << grossPay << endl;

        cout << "\nFIT WH\t\tFICA WH\t\tState WH";
        cout << "\n======\t\t=======\t\t========";
        cout << "\n" << fitAmt << "\t\t" << ficaAmt << "\t\t" << stateAmt << endl;
        cout << "\nLocal WH\tMed. Ins.\tTotal Ded.";
        cout << "\n========\t=========\t==========";
        cout << "\n" << localAmt << "\t\t" << medIns << "\t\t" << totDed << endl;

        cout << "\nNet Pay";
        cout << "\n=======";
        cout << "\n" << netPay << "\n\n";


        // Prompt the user to continue
        cout << "\nWould you like to enter another employee?";
        cout << "\nEnter 1 for Yes, 2 for No:   ";
        cin >> answer;

        if (answer != 1)
            break;

        else
            continue;
    }


        // End the main function
        return 0;
}


unsigned int hoursEntry()
{

        unsigned int sunHrs = 0, monHrs = 0, tueHrs = 0, wedHrs = 0;
        unsigned int thuHrs = 0, friHrs = 0, satHrs = 0;
        unsigned int tHrs = 0;

        // Begin getting info from user
        cout << "Enter hours worked for each day.\n";
        cout << "Enter 0 if no hours worked.\n";

        cout << "\nSunday Hours: ";
        cin >> sunHrs;
        tHrs = sunHrs;

        cout << "\nMonday hours: ";
        cin >> monHrs;
```

```cpp
    tHrs += monHrs;

    cout << "\nTuesday Hours: ";
    cin >> tueHrs;
    tHrs += tueHrs;

    cout << "\nWednesday hours: ";
    cin >> wedHrs;
    tHrs += wedHrs;

    cout << "\nThursday Hours: ";
    cin >> thuHrs;
    tHrs += thuHrs;

    cout << "\nFriday hours: ";
    cin >> friHrs;
    tHrs += friHrs;

    cout << "\nSaturday hours: ";
    cin >> satHrs;
    tHrs += satHrs;

    return tHrs;
}


double FIT(int mStat)
{
    double fWH;

    // Decide on  FIT percent based on marital status
    if (mStat == 1)
            fWH = .20;
    else if (mStat == 2)
            fWH = .15;
    else
        {
            fWH = 0;
            cout << "\nFIT Error";
        }

    return fWH;
}


double MED(int mStat)
{
    double mIns;

    // Calculate medical insurance
    if (mStat == 1)
            mIns = 10.00;
    else if (mStat == 2)
            mIns = 18.00;
```

```
        else
          {
              mIns = 0;
              cout << "\nMedical Insurance Error";
          }
      return mIns;
}
```

You now have a program that allows the user to calculate payroll for an unlimited number of employees. This program is very similar to a regular payroll program, it's just simpler! You are now capable of creating a multitude of programs. The only limitation is your imagination!

Summary

In this lesson, you learned how to integrate the programming tools and code that you learned about in earlier lessons, into a reliable payroll program. You began by designing a payroll program using flowcharts, pseudocode, or narratives. Then, you separated the program into logical themes so that you could create functions.

Finally, you looped the program so that the user could input multiple employees for which to calculate payroll. This allowed the program to operate in a way similar to a more sophisticated payroll program.

LESSON 6 REVIEW QUESTIONS

SHORT ANSWER

Define the following in the space provided.

1. User interaction

   _____

2. User interface

   _____

3. Calculations

   _____

4. Control structures

   _____

5. Sequence control structure

_____

6. Selection control structure

_____

7. Repetition control structure

_____

8. Top-down programming

_____

_____

9. if

_____

_____

10. if/else

_____

_____

11. switch

_____

_____

12. looping

_____

13. while

_____

_____

14. do/while

_____

_____

15. for

_____

_____

16. counter

_____

17. Initialized

_____

18. Increment

_____

19. Function prototype

_____

20. Function call

_____

21. Function definition

_____

22. Header file

_____

_____

23. EOF character

_____

_____

24. Endless loop

_____

WRITTEN QUESTIONS

Write your answers to the following questions in the space provided.

1. Why are functions used?

_____

_____

_____

2. Describe the appropriate size for a function.

_____

3. Explain the benefit of using a header file.

_____

_____

4. Explain how selection structures provide control to the user.

_____

5. Explain how repetition structures provide control to the user.

_____

6. Explain the use of flowcharts, pseudocode, and narratives.

_____

7. Explain the concept of "user friendly."

_____

8. Explain how all the concepts you've learned in the first 6 lessons of this book interact with each other.

_____

_____

_____

_____

_____

9. Explain why the following sequence of code will not make a good function.

```
//Separate the hours into regular and overtime
if (totHrs <= 40)
    regHrs = totHrs;
else {
    regHrs = 40;
    otHrs = totHrs - 40;
}
```

_____

_____

TESTING YOUR SKILLS

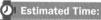 **Estimated Time:**

APPLICATION 6-1

Application 6-1 30 minutes
Application 6-2 1 ^{1}/$_2$ hours
Application 6-3 1 ^{1}/$_4$ hours

Create a title header for your payroll input screen. Use **Project 6-1B.cpp** as the basis for this application. Save your file as **App6-1.cpp**.

APPLICATION 6-2

Add code to your program that will allow the user to enter a user first name and last name for each employee. Also, make sure the employee's first and last name display to the screen when the payroll information is displayed at the end of the program. Use **Project 6-1B.cpp** as the basis for this application. Save your file as **App6-2.cpp**.

APPLICATION 6-3

Attempt to create a function for the output section of your payroll program. Use **Project 6-1B.cpp** as the basis for this application. If you are unable to create a function, then write a brief explanation as to why you cannot. Save the file as **App6-3.cpp** regardless of whether or not you could create the function.

CRITICAL THINKING

Estimated Time: 2 hours

Smaller functions are sometimes better implemented as *inline functions*. Inline functions reduce processing time because they eliminate function calls. In place of function calls, the compiler places the code for the inline function into your program where you place the function (not the function definition). Therefore, the trade-off is additional lines of code vs. additional processing time.

Modify your **Project 6-1B.cpp** code so that the following lines of code are rewritten as inline functions. Save the modified file as **Crit6-4.cpp**.

1. regPay = regHrs * hrlyrate;

2. otPay = otHrs * hrlyRate * 1.5;

3. grossPay = regPay + otPay;

When you are finished, explain why these lines of code are probably best left alone and not made into any kind of function.

_____

_____

_____

_____

_____

BASIC DATA MANIPULATION

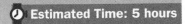

OBJECTIVES

Upon completion of this lesson, you should be able to:

- Explain arrays.

- Declare and initialize arrays.

- Display array output in columns.

- Select array elements using subscripts and pointers.

- Set array size using a constant variable.

- Sort data in both ascending and descending order.

- Perform linear searches.

🕐 **Estimated Time: 5 hours**

Introduction

Data manipulation is a very important part of computer programming. In fact, there are probably very few, if any, application programs available that do not offer the user the choice of some sort of data manipulation. One of the most important aspects of data manipulation is the ability to store and retrieve information. In this lesson temporary storage and data manipulation will be discussed.

Arrays are a group of consecutive memory locations that all have the same name and same data type. They are useful for temporarily storing data to be manipulated. With arrays you can structure the data that is input, basically placing the data in "locations" within a "table." You can then access the data by *referencing* its address with a pointer, or by explicitly going to its location using a subscript. Both methods are acceptable, but the pointer will provide you with more powerful ways of doing things down the road.

A *pointer* is simply a variable that is created to hold a *memory address*. You can then access data by providing the pointer variable with an *explicit* or *implicit address*. A *subscript*, on the other hand, is simply the number of the *element*, or item, in the array. Even though subscripts are simple, they can cause some confusion.

Arrays start numbering their elements, or items, with *zero*. So the first element in an array is *not* element 1, but element zero. So, if you are looking for the sixth item in the array, it would be subscript 5 (0, 1, 2, 3, 4, **5**). This confusion sometimes leads to *off-by-one errors*. If you want to display the contents of item 6, you need to ask for subscript 5. If you ask for subscript 6, you will actually get the seventh item in the array. One way to avoid this problem is to remember that every time you are looking for a specific element, the subscript becomes the element you are looking for *minus 1*.

Arrays are also useful in compiling results, such as you did with the simple survey created in Project 5-5, and in sorting data. This lesson will focus on the following:

■ **Declaring and initializing arrays.** You will be creating arrays and showing various ways to initialize them.

■ **Displaying array output in columns.** You will be including output manipulators to make array data display in columns. This simply gives you the output in a format most people like to see when dealing with data.

■ **Setting array size using a constant variable.** One of the best ways to initialize a variable is to use a *constant variable*. A constant variable lets you change the array size by changing the value of the constant variable. This method results in your programs being coded clearer and executing faster.

■ **Selecting array elements using subscripts and pointers.** Both of these tools will prove to be useful in your programming endeavors. So make sure you use both methods in this lesson.

■ **Sorting data in ascending and descending order.** *Sorting* data is very important in computer applications, especially in database activities. Data is stored in a computer usually in the order it is entered. You need to be able to reorder the data so that it is in a more logical sequence, depending on the application. For example, a personal phone book would be much easier to use if it was in alphabetical order by last name. You'll take a look at sorting data in both *ascending* and *descending* order.

■ **Performing linear searches.** Searching for data is important, especially in the areas of database administration and Web site administration. Think about how much time you spend looking for things, and then think about how helpful it would be if you could create the ultimate search program!

Arrays—here we come!

PROJECT 7-1 : Simple Array Ⓑ

In this project, you will declare and initialize a simple array.

Step 1: Start Your Compiler

Start your compiler if it is not already running.

Step 2: Type in Your Code

Your code should be typed in exactly as follows. Save this program as **Project 7-1.cpp**. Remember to save your code after typing in the first line or two of your program, and then as often as possible thereafter.

```
#include <iostream.h>

main()
{
    int element;
    int simpleArray[10] = {1, 3, 5, 7, 9, 11, 13, 15, 17, 19};

    for (element = 0; element < 10; element++)
        cout << "Element # " << element << " holds the value "
        << simpleArray[element] << "\n";

    return 0;
}
```

Step 3: Save Your Program

Once you have finished typing in your code, save your code one final time before compiling your program.

Step 4: Build, Link, Run

Enter the commands necessary to build, link, and run your program. If errors occur during any of these processes, check your code, correct any errors, and rerun the program.

You should have 10 lines displayed on your screen that look like the following:

```
Element #0 holds the value 1

Element #1 holds the value 3

Element #2 holds the value 5

Element #3 holds the value 7

Element #4 holds the value 9

Element #5 holds the value 11

Element #6 holds the value 13

Element #7 holds the value 15

Element #8 holds the value 17

Element #9 holds the value 19

Press any key to continue
```

Step 5: Explain Your Code

You've taken the above code and broken it into blocks.

1. In the space below, explain the following block of code.

```
main()
{
    int element;
    int simpleArray[10] = {1, 3, 5, 7, 9, 11, 13, 15, 17, 19};
```

_____

_____

_____

_____

_____

You should recognize that this section of code begins the main function. You then have the opening brace of the main function. Then you have two integer declarations. The first simply sets up an integer variable named "element." The second declares an array variable with 10 elements and then initializes the array with the set of numbers that follows.

You will notice that the size of the array is contained in brackets and the elements are contained in braces, separated by commas.

2. Explain the *for* statement in the following block of code.

```
for (element = 0; element < 10; element++)
    cout << "Element # " << element << " holds the value "
    << simpleArray[element] << "\n";
```

_____

_____

_____

You should recognize that the *for* statement initializes the "element" variable to a value of 0. Then it causes a loop to execute as long as the value of the "element" variable is less than 10. After each repetition of the loop, the "element" variable is incremented by 1 (postincrement).

3. Explain why the loop condition is less than 10.

_____

_____

_____

Since there are 10 elements in the array you would think that the loop condition should be less than 11. However, arrays begin counting with zero; therefore, the highest element number is 9, which is less than 10.

4. Explain the command that is performed each time through the *for* loop.

_____

_____

Each time through the loop a line is displayed to the screen that reads:

'Element # x holds the value x'

5. What benefit does using the element variable provide to you?

_____

_____

_____

P R O J E C T   7 - 2 : Formatting Array Output Ⓑ

Before you move any further into arrays, investigate how to format your output. Since most users expect output in some sort of report form, you will learn how to format your output in a columnar format.

Step 1: Start Your Compiler

Start your compiler if it is not already running.

Step 2: Open the Project 7-1.cpp File

Open the **Project 7-1.cpp** file, and save it as **Project 7-2.cpp**.

Step 3: Modify Your Code

Modify your code so that it looks exactly like the code shown below.

```
#include <iostream.h>
#include <iomanip.h>

main()
{
    int element;
    int simpleArray[10] = {1, 3, 5, 7, 9, 11, 13, 15, 17, 19};

    cout << "Element #" << setw(9) << "Value" << "\n";

    for (element = 0; element < 10; element++)
        cout << setw(9) << element << setw(9)
        << simpleArray[element] << "\n";

    return 0;
}
```

Step 4: Save Your Program

Once you have finished typing in your code, save your code one final time before compiling your program.

Step 5: Build, Link, Run

Enter the commands necessary to build, link, and run your program. If errors occur during any of these processes, check your code, correct any errors, and rerun the program.

You should have 12 lines displayed on your screen that look like the following:

```
Element #    Value

    0          1

    1          3

    2          5

    3          7

    4          9

    5         11

    6         13

    7         15

    8         17

    9         19

Press any key to continue
```

Step 6: Explain Your Code

Now take a look at your modifications.

1. In the space below, explain why you need to include the *iomanip.h* file, as shown in the block of code below.

```
#include <iostream.h>
#include <iomanip.h>
```

_____

_____

2. Explain the setw stream manipulator in the block of code below.

```
cout << setw(9) << element << setw(9)
<< simpleArray[element] << "\n";
```

So there you have it—a simple array and formatted columnar output. Now explore some more challenging aspects of arrays.

PROJECT 7 - 3 : Pointers

Pointers are a very important part of programming, but they are somewhat difficult to grasp. Basically, a pointer is a variable that points at an address. Therefore, when you use a pointer to find an array element, you are simply finding the address of the memory area in which the element value is stored. Then, from that memory address, you are able to access the element value.

Try a project that uses pointers instead of subscripts, as you've been doing.

Step 1: Start Your Compiler

Start your compiler if it is not already running.

Step 2: Open the Project 7-2.cpp File

Open the **Project 7-2.cpp** file, and save it as **Project 7-3.cpp**.

Step 3: Modify Your Code

Modify your code so that it looks exactly like the code shown below.

```
#include <iostream.h>
#include <iomanip.h>

main()
{
    int element;
    int *elementPtr;
    int simpleArray[10] = {1, 3, 5, 7, 9, 11, 13, 15, 17, 19};

    cout << "Element #" << setw(9) << "Value" << setw(15) << "Address\n";

    for (element = 0; element < 10; element++)
        {
         elementPtr = &simpleArray[element];
         cout << setw(9) << element << setw(9)
         << *elementPtr << setw(15) << elementPtr << "\n";
        }
    return 0;
}
```

Step 4: Save Your Program

Once you have finished typing in your code, save your code one final time before compiling your program.

Step 5: Build, Link, Run

Enter the commands necessary to build, link, and run your program. If errors occur during any of these processes, check your code, correct any errors, and rerun the program.

You should have 12 lines displayed on your screen that look like the following:

```
Element #    Value       Address

      0        1       0x0065FDC8

      1        3       0x0065FDCC

      2        5       0x0065FDD0

      3        7       0x0065FDD4

      4        9       0x0065FDD8

      5       11       0x0065FDDC

      6       13       0x0065FDE0

      7       15       0x0065FDE4

      8       17       0x0065FDE8

      9       19       0x0065FDEC

Press any key to continue
```

 HOT TIP

The address values will vary from computer system to computer system.

Step 6: Review Your Code

Now take a look at your modifications.

1. Explain the three lines of code in the block below, and their relationship to each other.

```
{
    int element;
    int *elementPtr;
    int simpleArray[10] = {1, 3, 5, 7, 9, 11, 13, 15, 17, 19};
```

_____

_____

_____

_____

_____

_____

2. Explain the following output line.

```
cout << "Element #" << setw(9) << "Value" << setw(15) << "Address\n";
```

_____

_____

_____

3. Explain the following for statement.

```
for (element = 0; element < 10; element++)
```

_____

_____

_____

4. Explain the following assignment.

```
elementPtr = &simpleArray[element];
```

_____

_____

_____

_____

_____

5. Explain the values that will be displayed due to the variables used in the code below.

```
cout << setw(9) << element << setw(9)
<< *elementPtr << setw(15) << elementPtr << "\n";
```

_____

_____

_____

_____

_____

_____

At this point, discuss your programs with your teacher and classmates to reinforce your understanding of the projects you've finished. You should now be able to create arrays and reference the values in those arrays.

Arrays usually do not initialize themselves. Nor does the programmer initialize arrays. It is the user that determines which data needs to be in the array. In this project, you will create a loop that allows the user to input the numbers needed.

Step 1: Start Your Compiler

Start your compiler if it is not already running.

Step 2: Open the Project 7-2.cpp File

Open your **Project 7-2.cpp** file, and save it as **Project 7-4.cpp**.

Step 3: Modify Your Code

Modify your code so that it looks exactly like the code shown below.

```cpp
#include <iostream.h>
#include <iomanip.h>

main()
{
    int element;
    int value;
    int simpleArray[10];

    cout << "Please enter 10 numbers.\n";

    for (element = 0; element < 10; element++)
        {
         cout << "\nEnter a number: ";
         cin >> value;
         simpleArray[element] = value;
        }


    cout << "Element #" << setw(9) << "Value" << "\n";

    for (element = 0; element < 10; element++)
        cout << setw(9) << element << setw(9)
        << simpleArray[element] << "\n";

    return 0;
}
```

Step 4: Save Your Program

Once you have finished typing in your code, save your code one final time before compiling your program.

Step 5: Build, Link, Run

Enter the commands necessary to build, link, and run your program. If errors occur during any of these processes, check your code, correct any errors, and rerun the program.

Your program should ask you for 10 numbers, although not specifically. However, after the 10th number is input, the program continues on with its execution. The result is that you should have 12 lines displayed on your screen that look like the following. Of course, your values will differ depending on your input.

```
Element #    Value

       0        1

       1        3

       2        5

       3        7

       4        9

       5       11

       6       13

       7       15

       8       17

       9       19

Press any key to continue
```

Have you noticed that this output is very similar to the output from Project 7-2? The only difference is the values.

Step 6: Review Your Code

Now take a look at your modifications.

1. Explain the execution of the loop shown in the code below and the purpose it serves.

```
cout << "Please enter 10 numbers.\n";

for (element = 0; element < 10; element++)
    {
```

```
cout << "\nEnter a number: ";
cin >> value;
simpleArray[element] = value;
}
```

_____

_____

_____

_____

2. You added one additional line of code. Write down that line and then explain the effect on the program if the line had *not* been added.

_____

_____

_____

When you're finished, discuss your answers with your teacher and classmates to reinforce your ability to analyze C++ code.

It's important to know how arrays can be initialized both by the programmer and by the user. The loop used in this project allows you to have the user input the data required.

PROJECT 7-5:
Using a Constant Variable to Set Array Size

(B)

This project is short and sweet, but *important!* Constant variables can be used to initialize array size. By using a constant variable you can make your program much more scaleable. If you would like an array size to increase from 10 to 350, or to 150,000, then you only need to change the value assigned to the constant variable! By using the constant variable in the remainder of your code, in the places where the array size is needed, the change takes care of itself! You simply change the value of the constant variable and every place it's used, the new value is automatically inserted.

Step 1: Start Your Compiler

Start your compiler if it is not already running.

Step 2: Open the Project 7-2.cpp File

Open your **Project 7-2.cpp** file, and save it as **Project 7-5.cpp**.

Step 3: Modify Your Code

Modify your code so that it looks exactly like the code shown below.

174

```
#include <iostream.h>
#include <iomanip.h>

main()
{
    int element;
    const int arraySize = 10;
    int simpleArray[arraySize] = {1, 3, 5, 7, 9, 11, 13, 15, 17, 19};

    cout << "Element #" << setw(9) << "Value" << "\n";

    for (element = 0; element < arraySize; element++)
        cout << setw(9) << element << setw(9)
        << simpleArray[element] << "\n";

    return 0;
}
```

Step 4: Save Your Program

Once you have finished typing in your code, save your code one final time before compiling your program.

Step 5: Build, Link, Run

Enter the commands necessary to build, link, and run your program. If errors occur during any of these processes, check your code, correct any errors, and rerun the program.

Your output should look exactly like the output from Project 7-2.

Step 6: Review Your Code

Explain what was accomplished by modifying the code.

1. Write down each line of code that was modified. Explain each modification.

_____

_____

_____

_____

_____

_____

_____

_____

_____

_____

When you're finished, discuss your answers with your teacher and classmates to reinforce your ability to analyze C++ code.

PROJECT 7-6:
Compiling Survey Results Using Two Arrays

(B)

In this project, you're going to use two arrays to compile and display survey results. This is an extremely useful application for arrays. You're giving the user control over inputting the results collected into one array; then, you accumulate the results into another array, and display the results to screen.

Step 1: Start Your Compiler

Start your compiler if it is not already running.

Step 2: Open the Project 7-4.cpp File

Open your **Project 7-4.cpp** file, and save it as **Project 7-6.cpp**.

Step 3: Modify Your Code

Modify your code so that it looks exactly like the code shown below.

```cpp
#include <iostream.h>
#include <iomanip.h>

main()
{
    int element;
    int value;
    const int arraySize = 20;
    const int responseSize = 4;
    int simpleArray[arraySize];
    int responseArray[responseSize] = {0};

    cout << "Please enter your survey results.\n";
    cout << "\nEnter 1- Agree, 2- Disagree, 3 - No Opinion\n";

    for (element = 0; element < arraySize; element++)
        {
         cout << "\nEnter a result: ";
         cin >> value;
         simpleArray[element] = value;
        }

    for (element = 0; element < arraySize; element++)
        {
         if (simpleArray[element] == 1)
            {
             value = 1;
```

```
                    ++responseArray[value];
                }
            else if (simpleArray[element] == 2)
                {
                 value = 2;
                 ++responseArray[value];
                }
            else if (simpleArray[element] == 3)
                {
                 value = 3;
                 ++responseArray[value];
                }
        }


    cout << "Response" << setw(15) << "Number of" << "\n";

    for (value = 1; value < responseSize; value++)
        cout << setw(8) << value << setw(15)
        << responseArray[value] << "\n";

    return 0;
}
```

Step 4: Save Your Program

Once you have finished typing in your code, save your code one final time before compiling your program.

Step 5: Build, Link, Run

Enter the commands necessary to build, link, and run your program. If errors occur during any of these processes, check your code, correct any errors, and rerun the program.

Your output should look exactly like the output from Project 7-2.

Step 6: Review Your Code

Explain what was accomplished by modifying the code.

1. Explain the following block of code.

```
cout << "Please enter your survey results.\n";
cout << "\nEnter 1- Agree, 2- Disagree, 3 - No Opinion\n";

for (element = 0; element < arraySize; element++)
    {
     cout << "\nEnter a result: ";
     cin >> value;
     simpleArray[element] = value;
    }
```

2. Explain the following block of code.

```
for (element = 0; element < arraySize; element++)
 {
  if (simpleArray[element] == 1)
     {
      value = 1;
      ++responseArray[value];
     }
  else if (simpleArray[element] == 2)
     {
      value = 2;
      ++responseArray[value];
     }
  else if (simpleArray[element] == 3)
     {
      value = 3;
      ++responseArray[value];
     }
 }
```

_____

_____

_____

_____

3. Do the *for* statements in the block of code above conflict with each other? Explain your answer.

_____

_____

4. Explain each of the declared items shown in the code below. Identify what they are, their type, and any values assigned to them.

```
int element;
int value;
const int arraySize = 20;
const int responseSize = 4;
int simpleArray[arraySize];
int responseArray[responseSize] = {0};
```

_____

_____

_____

_____

_____

5. What purpose do each of the items in #4 serve in your program?

_____

_____

_____

_____

6. Explain the following block of code.

```
cout << "Response" << setw(15) << "Number of" << "\n";

for (value = 1; value < responseSize; value++)
    cout << setw(8) << value << setw(15)
         << responseArray[value] << "\n";
```

_____

_____

When you're finished, discuss your answers with your teacher and classmates to reinforce your ability to analyze C++ code.

You're well on your way to mastering arrays!

PROJECT 7 - 7 : Bubble Sort

Another important need of programmers and users is to be able to sort data. Collecting the data and storing it is only part of the solution. You need to be able to put the data in a logical, practical order. The **bubble sort** is an easy solution to sorting. Although it will run slowly when used with large arrays, it will serve our needs for the time being. The reason this type of sort is called a bubble sort is that with each pass through the sorting loop, the smaller numbers "bubble" their way to the top.

Sorting is attracting some of the most intensive research in data processing today. That's because almost every institution has data it needs to sort.

Step 1: Start Your Compiler

Start your compiler if it is not already running.

Step 2: Open the Project 7-4.cpp File

Open your **Project 7-4.cpp** file, and save it as **Project 7-7.cpp**.

Step 3: Modify Your Code

Modify your code so that it looks exactly like the code shown on the next page.

```
// Project 7-7 (Modified from Project 7-4)
// Programmer: <Your Name>
// Bubble Sort

#include <iostream.h>
#include <iomanip.h>

main()
{
    int element;
    int value;
    int swap;
    int loops;
    const int arraySize = 10;
    int simpleArray[arraySize];


    // This allows the user to input the array elements
    cout << "Please enter 10 numbers.\n";

    for (element = 0; element < arraySize; element++)
        {
        cout << "\nEnter a number: ";
        cin >> value;
        simpleArray[element] = value;
        }


    // This prints out the value of each element in the original order
    cout << "Unsorted Items\n";
    cout << "==============\n";
    cout << "Element #" << setw(9) << "Value" << "\n";

    for (element = 0; element < arraySize; element++)
        cout << setw(9) << element << setw(9)
        << simpleArray[element] << "\n";


    // This is where you do the bubble sort
    for (loops = 0; loops < arraySize -1; loops++)

        for (element = 0; element < arraySize -1 ; element++)
            if (simpleArray[element] > simpleArray [element + 1])
                {
                swap = simpleArray[element];
                simpleArray[element] = simpleArray[element + 1];
                simpleArray[element + 1] = swap;
                }
```

```
    // This is where you display the sorted items
    cout << "Sorted Items\n";
    cout << "==============\n";
    cout << "Element #" << setw(9) << "Value" << "\n";

    for (element = 0; element < 10; element++)
        cout << setw(9) << element << setw(9)
        << simpleArray[element] << "\n";



    return 0;
}
```

Step 4: Save Your Program

Once you have finished typing in your code, save your code one final time before compiling your program.

Step 5: Build, Link, Run

Enter the commands necessary to build, link, and run your program. If errors occur during any of these processes, check your code, correct any errors, and rerun the program.

The first part of your output should look exactly like the output from Project 7-4. The second part should look similar, with one exception—the values should be in *ascending* order.

Step 6: Review Your Code

Explain what was accomplished by modifying the code.

1. Write down the items from the block of code shown below that have been modified from Project 7-4 or are new to this project. Explain the purpose of the modifications or the additions.

```
int element;
int value;
int swap;
int loops;
const int arraySize = 10;
int simpleArray[arraySize];
```

_____

_____

_____

2. The following block of code is your entire bubble sort. Explain why two *for* statements are used.

```
// This is where you do the bubble sort
for (loops = 0; loops < arraySize -1; loops++)

    for (element = 0; element < arraySize -1 ; element++)
```

```
if (simpleArray[element] > simpleArray [element + 1])
   {
    swap = simpleArray[element];
    simpleArray[element] = simpleArray[element + 1];
    simpleArray[element + 1] = swap;
   }
```

_____

_____

_____

3. Explain the body of the nested *for* statement.

_____

_____

4. Explain the *swap* variable.

_____

_____

5. Explain the *loops* variable.

_____

_____

When you're finished, discuss your answers with your teacher and classmates to reinforce your ability to analyze C++ code.

Now you are capable of coding bubble sorts!

PROJECT 7-8 : Searching Ⓑ

Another important need of programmers and users is to be able to find data. In this project, you will learn how to perform a simple ***linear search***. This type of search works well with small and unsorted arrays. However, for large arrays, linear searching is inefficient; for these you will need to develop a ***binary search*** method.

Step 1: Start Your Compiler

Start your compiler if it is not already running.

Step 2: Open the Project 7-4.cpp File

Open your **Project 7-4.cpp** file, and save it as **Project 7-8.cpp**.

Step 3: Modify Your Code

Modify your code so that it looks exactly like the code shown below.

```cpp
// Project 7-8 (Was Project 7-4)
// Programmer: <Your Name>
// Linear Search

#include <iostream.h>

main()
{
    int element;
    int value;
    int searcher;
    int found = -1;
    int foundElement;
    const int arraySize = 10;
    int simpleArray[arraySize];

    cout << "Please enter 10 numbers.\n";

    for (element = 0; element < arraySize; element++)
        {
         cout << "\nEnter a number: ";
         cin >> value;
         simpleArray[element] = value;
        }


    cout << "\nWhich number are you searching for? ";
    cin >> searcher;

    for (element = 0; element < arraySize; element++)
        {
         if (simpleArray[element] == searcher)
            {
             found = simpleArray[element];
             foundElement = element;
             element = arraySize;
            }
        }

    if (found != -1)
        cout << "\nThe number you are looking for " << searcher
            << " is in element " << foundElement << ".\n";
    else
        cout << "\nThe number you are looking for " << searcher
            << " was not found.\n";

    return 0;
}
```

Step 4: Save Your Program

Once you have finished typing in your code, save your code one final time before compiling your program.

Step 5: Build, Link, Run

Enter the commands necessary to build, link, and run your program. If errors occur during any of these processes, check your code, correct any errors, and rerun the program.

The input should look exactly like that from Project 7-4. The second part should return the value for which you searched, or it will tell you if the value was *not* found.

Step 6: Review Your Code

Explain what was accomplished by modifying the code.

1. Explain the following two lines of code.

```
cout << "\nWhich number are you searching for? ";
cin >> searcher;
```

_____

2. The block of code below is the entire linear search. Explain this block of code.

```
for (element = 0; element < arraySize; element++)
    {
     if (simpleArray[element] == searcher)
        {
         found = simpleArray[element];
         foundElement = element;
         element = arraySize;
        }
    }
```

_____

_____

_____

_____

3. Explain the block of code below.

```
if (found != -1)
    cout << "\nThe number you are looking for " << searcher
         << " is in element " << foundElement << ".\n";
else
    cout << "\nThe number you are looking for " << searcher
         << " was not found.\n";
```

_____

_____

_____

_____

When you're finished, discuss your answers with your teacher and classmates to reinforce your ability to analyze C++ code.

Now you are capable of coding linear searches!

Summary

This lesson was an overview of a number of useful data manipulation tools. You learned how to create an array, and then how to format the output so that it's easy to read and interpret.

Pointers and their importance to programming were discussed. You learned that you could reference data indirectly by referencing the memory address of the data. Pointers are created for just that purpose—to point at memory addresses. The project you created for pointers showed how easy it is to use these to get to your data.

Initializing the array is very important. You saw the fact that the user may need to input the data to be manipulated. Then, you created a loop that allowed the user to input the data collected for your program. You also discovered that the size of the array needs to be set before the array is compiled. The reason for this is that the compiler sets aside a specific amount of memory for the array. By using a constant variable, you were able to add scalability to your program. In other words, if the array ever needed to change size, all you would need to modify is the value of the constant variable. You then learned about manipulation. The first pure manipulation you performed was a bubble sort. Bubble sorts are an easy way to put your data in either ascending or descending order. You learned how important it is for a user to be able to access data, often in a specific order. Banks, for instance, put checks from your checking account into ascending order. Direct mail organizations sort their outgoing mailings by ZIP code in order to get reduced postage rates. So you can see the importance of sorting.

And, finally, you performed a simple linear search. You learned that linear searches are useful in small, unsorted arrays. Binary searching is more practical for larger arrays.

LESSON 7 REVIEW QUESTIONS

SHORT ANSWER

Define the following in the space provided.

1. Arrays

_____

2. Referencing

_____

_____

3. Memory address

_____

4. Pointer

_____

5. Subscript

_____

6. Explicitly

_____

7. Implicitly

_____

8. Element

_____

9. Constant variable

_____

10. Database

_____

11. Linear search

_____

_____

12. Binary search

_____

13. while

_____

14. setw

_____

15. Indirection operator (*)

_____

_____

16. Address operator (&)

_____

_____

17. Bubble sort

_____

_____

18. Sort

_____

19. Ascending

_____

20. Descending

_____

21. Scaleability

_____

_____

22. Compiled

_____

WRITTEN QUESTIONS

Write your answers to the following questions in the space provided.

1. Explain off-by-one errors.

_____

_____

2. Explain the benefit of using a constant variable to set the size of an array.

_____

_____

_____

3. Explain why the number of the first element in an array is zero.

_____

4. Explain the difference between the value returned from a pointer variable when using the indirection operator and when *not* using the indirection operator.

_____

_____

5. Explain the need to use the *iomanip.h* file when using output manipulators.

_____

_____

6. Explain the difference between a linear search and a binary search.

_____

_____

7. Explain sorting.

_____

8. Explain how a bubble sort works.

_____

_____

_____

_____

9. Explain the purpose of using the swap variable in the bubble sort in Project 7-7.

_____

_____

TESTING YOUR SKILLS

Estimated Time:
Application 7-1 30 minutes
Application 7-2 1 hour
Application 7-3 2 hours

APPLICATION 7-1

Using your **Project 7-7.cpp** file, modify the code to create a *descending* order bubble sort. Save your file as **App7-1.cpp**.

APPLICATION 7-2

Modify your **Project 7-8** program so that the entire program you coded becomes a separate function. Use the **Project 7-8.cpp** file as the basis for this application. Save your file as **App7-2.cpp**.

APPLICATION 7-3

Create three separate functions for your **Project 7-7** survey results program. In your original program you allowed the user to enter survey results, then your program displayed the compiled results by answer. Now, add three separate functions: calculate and display the mean (average), the median (the middle number), and the mode (the answer that appears the most often). Use **Project 7-7.cpp** as the basis for this application. Save your file as **App7-3.cpp**.

CRITICAL THINKING

Estimated Time:
Activity 7-1 2 hours
Activity 7-2 2 hours

ACTIVITY 7-1

Create an array that accumulates, and then displays, the result of a random number generator that mimics the repetitive tossing of dice.

ACTIVITY 7-2

Create a binary search routine to use on a large, sorted array. Create a large array of at least 100 elements, populate the array with any method you choose, and then perform a binary search.

SIMPLE DATA STRUCTURES

LESSON

8

OBJECTIVES

Upon completion of this lesson, you should be able to:

■ Create a single subscript array.

■ Create a double subscript array.

■ Choose appropriate situations to use multiple subscript arrays.

■ Define and create a data structure.

■ Declare variables to be used in the structure.

■ Access structure members.

■ Create a simple class.

🕐 **Estimated Time: 4 hours**

Introduction

In Lesson 7 you learned how to create arrays, declare and use pointers, and perform a bubble sort and a linear search. Arrays represent a simple, easy way to store information. However, they can be limited. Arrays occupy a specific amount of space in memory and you need to reserve the amount of memory that the array will use. You have to specify the memory up front, when you *declare* the size of the array. If the array needs to be bigger, then you have to create a new array and move the existing data into it.

This lesson will concentrate on creating and using simple data structures, which will include a quick review of single subscript arrays. Single subscript arrays have one long "row" of information—period. You will expand from single subscript arrays into *multiple subscript arrays*. You will also create and use an array with two subscripts. This will effectively provide a storage structure that contains both *rows* and *columns*, similar to a spreadsheet. Most C++ compilers support up to 12 subscripts.

You will then revisit the C notion of *struct*—the structure. *Structures* provide a way to create an *aggregate data type* using data of other types. Both the benefits and drawbacks of using a structure will be discussed. You will also see how to access structure members using the *dot operator/member access operator*. The use of *struct* will lead you into creating a simple *class*. A class is a user-defined type that contains data as well as functions. The class is what is known as an *object*, and it forms the unit of programming in C++. Classes will be discussed further in Lesson 9.

This lesson will focus on the following:

■ **Creating a single subscript array.** You will review basically what you learned in Lesson 7.

191

- **Creating a double subscript array and determining when to use a multiple subscript array.** As explained above, double subscript arrays provide a storage structure that consists of rows and columns, similar to a spreadsheet or a database table. You will create and manipulate a double subscript array.

- **Defining and creating a data structure, declaring variables to be used in structures, and accessing structure members.** Structures are the predominant programming unit used in C. Understanding a structure is the first step in understanding a class, which is the programming unit in C++. In this lesson, you will create and manipulate a structure.

- **Creating a simple class.** This lesson will introduce you to the C++ unit of programming. Classes contain both data members and member functions, making them an object or a reusable data type.

P R O J E C T   8 - 1 : Single Subscript Array

This project is a simple review of the arrays you created in Lesson 7. Use this as a chance to review the basics of arrays and to get ready to apply your knowledge to more powerful arrays.

Step 1: Start Your Compiler

Start your compiler if it is not already running.

Step 2: Design Your Array

Create an array that will hold the ages of all the students in your class. You will need to create a user interface that allows a user to input all the students' ages. You will not include the ages when you declare the array. Use the questions below as a guide to lay out and code your program.

1. In the space below, write your main function.

_____

_____

_____

_____

_____

_____

_____

2. In the space below, add your user prompt for information. Make it user friendly. You will also probably need to use a *for* loop. The user input will be used to initialize the array.

_____

_____

_____

_____

_____

_____

_____

3. List the variables you will need for your program. Declare your array using a constant variable.

_____

_____

_____

_____

_____

_____

4. Create an output sequence that will display the element number and the value held in the element. Use a tabular format and put headings on each column.

_____

_____

_____

_____

_____

_____

_____

5. Write the comments that need to be inserted into your program.

_____

_____

_____

_____

_____

_____

_____

Step 3: Type in Your Code

Type your code in as you've written it above. Save it with the filename **Project 8-1.cpp**. Make sure you save your file often.

Step 4: Save Your Program

Once you have finished typing in your code, save your code one final time before compiling your program.

Step 5: Build, Link, Run

Enter the commands necessary to build, link, and run your program. If errors occur during any of these processes, check your code, correct any errors, and rerun the program.

Step 6: Review Your Code

Now that your program has run successfully, answer the following questions. Review your answers with your classmates and teacher.

1. How many header files did you need to use for your program to compile properly? List the header files you needed to use.

_____

_____

2. Explain the use of the constant variable in declaring your array.

_____

_____

3. Explain the purpose of the for loop used to input data.

_____

4. Explain how to create a tabular output.

_____

_____

Step 7: Check Your Code

If you have experienced some difficulty in designing and coding your program, or if you are simply curious to see how someone else may have coded the program, then review the sample code below. Remember, not everyone codes the same. Good programmers keep their eyes and ears open for new ways to code programs!

```cpp
// Project 8-1
// Simple Array Review

#include <iostream.h>
#include <iomanip.h>

main()
{
   int age;
   const int ageSize = 20;
   int ageArray[ageSize];

   cout << "Please enter the ages of your classmates.";
   cout << "\nThe data entry will end when you enter all ages.";

   for (int ctr = 0; ctr < ageSize; ctr++) {

      cout << "\n\nEnter an age: ";
      cin >> age;
      ageArray[ctr] = age;
   }

   cout << "\nThese are the ages you entered "
        << "and the element in which they are stored.";
   cout << "\nElement" << setw(9) << "Age";
   cout << "\n=======" << setw(9) << "===\n";


   for (ctr = 0; ctr < ageSize; ctr++) {
```

```
        cout << setw(7) << ctr << setw(9) << ageArray[ctr] <<        endl;
    }

    return 0;
}
```

Now, it's time to create a double subscript array.

P R O J E C T   8 - 2 : Double Subscript Array

Now that you've reviewed simple arrays, this project will expand on what you know.

There is not a great deal of difference between single and multiple subscript arrays, except that multiple subscripts add additional rows and columns to the array. They also use two subscript variables instead of one, and use embedded *for* loops to access information. In this project you will modify code from Project 8-1 into a double subscript array.

Step 1: Start Your Compiler

Start your compiler if it is not already running.

Step 2: Modify Your Code

Open your **Project 8-1.cpp** program file. Save it as **Project 8-2.cpp**.

Your Project 8-1 program used one input variable, one constant integer, one subscript for one array, one single *for* loop for input, and one single *for* loop for output. You should modify the Project 8-1 program as follows: For each student, you will record his or her age and grade level (for example, 10, 11, 12). Both numbers should be stored in a double subscripted array. Use constant variables to set the size of the array. Do not make the array too big until you are sure it works properly!

In order to get the numbers into the proper element, use an embedded *for* loop that uses both subscripts. You must also create some sort of cut-off test so that the user is prompted to enter grade levels instead of age. Your original program asks for age only. After you enter the age for each student, you will then need to repeat the process for grade level. Note that the user prompt will need to change. (*Hint:* Test for row number.) Once you have input all the information, you need to display it to see if it's correct. Your original display showed the element number and the age. Now you need to see an element number that consists of *two* subscripts, and then the age and the grade level. For simplicity, you may want to do two separate displays—one that shows the element number and the age, and then another that shows the element number and the grade level. You decide how fancy to get! Your output will probably use *for* loops.

Before you change the code, answer the questions below in order to assist you in properly modifying it.

1. How many input variables will you need for this program? Name them.

_____

2. How many constant integers should you use? Name them.

_____

195

3. How many subscripts will you need for your array? Name them.

_____

_____

4. In the space below, design and code the embedded *for* loops for your input sequence.

_____

_____

_____

_____

_____

_____

_____

_____

5. In the space below, design and code the output sequence.

_____

_____

_____

_____

_____

_____

_____

_____

6. In the space below, write and insert comments that explain each section of your program.

_____

_____

_____

_____

_____

_____

_____

_____

Step 3: Type in Your Code

Using the information from Step 2, type in your code. Make sure you save often.

Step 4: Build, Link, Run

Enter the commands necessary to build, link, and run your program. If errors occur during any of these processes, check your code, correct any errors, and rerun the program.

Make sure you test your program with "real" data to see if it executes properly.

Step 5: Review Your Code

Now that your program has run successfully, review your code with your classmates and teacher.

Step 6: Check Your Code

If you have experienced some difficulty in designing and coding your program, or if you are simply curious to see how someone else may have coded the program, then review the sample code below. Remember, not everyone codes the same. Good programmers keep their eyes and ears open for new ways to code programs!

```cpp
// Project 8-2
// Double Subscript Array

#include <iostream.h>
#include <iomanip.h>

main()
{
    int age, grade;
    const int rowSize = 2;
    const int colSize = 5;
    int ageArray[rowSize][colSize];

    cout << "Please enter the ages and grade level of your classmates.";
    cout << "\nThe data entry will end when you enter all ages and grade levels.";
    cout << "\nGrade levels means the grade number they are in.";

    for (int row = 0; row < rowSize; row++) {
        for (int col = 0; col < colSize; col++)
            if (row == 0){
                cout << "\n\nEnter an age: ";
                cin >> age;
                ageArray[row][col] = age;
            }
            else {
                cout << "\n\nEnter a grade level: ";
                cin >> grade;
                ageArray[row][col] = grade;
            }

    }

    cout << "\nThese are the ages you entered "
         << "and the element in which they are stored.";
    cout << "\nElement" << setw(9) << "Age";
    cout << "\n=======" << setw(9) << "===\n";
```

```
   row = 0;
   for (int col = 0; col < colSize; col++) {
      cout << row << ", " << col << setw(9) << ageArray[row][col] << endl;
   }

   cout << "\nThese are the grades you entered "
        << "and the element in which they are stored.";
   cout << "\nElement" << setw(9) << "Grade";
   cout << "\n=======" << setw(9) << "=====\n";

   row = 1;
   for (col = 0; col < colSize; col++) {
      cout << row << ", " << col << setw(9) << ageArray[row][col] << endl;
   }

   return 0;
}
```

You have now created and used a double subscript array. Your program may look different than the one shown above, but that's OK. Everyone has different ways to solve problems.

PROJECT 8 - 3 : Structures

You're now going to jump into structures. In this project, you will create a new data type from elements of other types.

Structures contain **members**. These members can be any type, but they are usually related to each other in some way. A structure cannot contain an **instance** of itself, but it can include a pointer to another structure of the same type. This will prove useful when **linking** data structures.

In this project you will define a structure and then use members of the structure to perform related functions.

Step 1: Start Your Compiler

Start your compiler if it is not already running.

Step 2: Type in Your Code

Type your code exactly as shown below. Save this program with the name **Project 8-3.cpp**. Remember to save your work as you type.

```
// Project 8-3.cpp
// Data structure

#include <iostream.h>

struct Car {
   int speed;
   int mpg;
   int fuel;
};
```

```
void printLecture(const Car &, int);

main()
{
    int speedLimit;
    int choice;

    Car fastCar;

    fastCar.speed = 75;
    fastCar.mpg = 12;
    fastCar.fuel = 20;


    Car slowCar;

    slowCar.speed = 35;
    slowCar.mpg = 48;
    slowCar.fuel = 20;

    cout << "Enter the speed limit of the road on which you are driving: \n";
    cin >> speedLimit;

    cout << "Are you driving a fast car or a slow car?\n";
    cout << "Enter 1 - Fast Car, or 2 - Slow Car: ";
    cin >> choice;


    if (choice == 1)
        printLecture(fastCar, speedLimit);
    else if (choice == 2)
        printLecture(slowCar, speedLimit);

    return 0;
}

void printLecture(const Car &c, int sl)
{
    if (sl < c.speed){
        cout << "You were speeding! You must drive slower!\n";
        cout << "You were driving " << c.speed - sl
            << " MPH over the speed limit!\n";
        cout << "Do you know that you will ONLY get "
            << c.mpg << " MPG at your speed?\n";
        cout << "If you have a " << c.fuel << " gallon gas tank"
            << " then you will only get " << c.mpg * c.fuel
            << " total miles!\n";
        cout << "Slow down!\n";
    }
    else if (sl >= c.speed){
        cout << "You drive as required by the law!\n";
        cout << "You will get better gas mileage that way!\n";
        cout << "With a " << c.fuel << " gallon gas tank "
            << "you should get approximately " << c.mpg * c.fuel
            << " total miles.\n";
```

```
    cout << "Good job!!\n";
  }
}
```

Step 3: Save Your Program

Once you have finished typing in your code, save it one final time before compiling the program.

Step 4: Build, Link, Run

Enter the commands necessary to build, link, and run your program. If errors occur during any of these processes, check your code, correct any errors, and rerun the program.

Step 5: Review Your Code

Now that your program has run successfully, review your code with your classmates and teacher.

1. In the space below, explain the following block of code.

```
struct Car {
   int speed;
   int mpg;
   int fuel;
};
```

_____

_____

_____

_____

_____

_____

2. What is the purpose of the following line of code?

```
void printLecture(const Car &, int);
```

_____

_____

_____

_____

_____

3. Explain the following block of code.

```
Car fastCar;

fastCar.speed = 75;
fastCar.mpg = 12;
fastCar.fuel = 20;
```

```
Car slowCar;

slowCar.speed = 35;
slowCar.mpg = 48;
slowCar.fuel = 20;
```

_____
_____
_____
_____
_____
_____

4. Explain the following if/else structure. Make sure you include mention of "passing by reference".

```
if (choice == 1)
   printLecture(fastCar, speedLimit);
else if (choice == 2)
   printLecture(slowCar, speedLimit);
```

_____
_____
_____
_____

5. Explain the use of structure members in the following function.

```
void printLecture(const Car &c, int sl)
{
   if (sl < c.speed){
      cout << "You were speeding! You must drive slower!\n";
      cout << "You were driving " << c.speed - sl
           << " MPH over the speed limit!\n";
      cout << "Do you know that you will ONLY get "
           << c.mpg << " MPG at your speed?\n";
      cout << "If you have a " << c.fuel << " gallon gas tank"
           << " then you will only get " << c.mpg * c.fuel
           << " total miles!\n";
      cout << "Slow down!\n";
   }
   else if (sl >= c.speed){
      cout << "You drive as required by the law!\n";
      cout << "You will get better gas mileage that way!\n";
      cout << "With a " << c.fuel << " gallon gas tank "
           << "you should get approximately " << c.mpg * c.fuel
           << " total miles.\n";
      cout << "Good job!!\n";
   }
}
```

_____
_____

_____

_____

_____

_____

_____

Step 7: Run Your Program

Run your program a few times to see what happens when you vary the speed limit and choose different cars. In reviewing your output you should notice any logic errors in your code. This program represents a very simple use of a structure. In the applications at the end of the lesson, you will be given a chance to modify this project.

PROJECT 8 - 4 : Self Referential Structure ⓘ

You will use the Project 8-3 program to complete this project. In discussing structures you learned that a structure *cannot* contain an **instance** of itself. This means that you cannot create another structure within the same type structure. However, you can create a **structure member** that points to another structure of the same type. This is useful in forming linked data structures.

In this program, it will prove useful because it allows you to access data members in other structures. You will be adding variables and a few lines of code in order to link to the slowCar structure.

Step 1: Start Your Compiler

If your compiler is not already running, start it now.

Step 2: Modify Your Code

Open your **Project 8-3.cpp** file. Modify your code as directed below. Save the program as **Project 8-4.cpp**. *Remember:* Save often as you type in the code. Add comments to your code as you enter it.

1. Add a pointer variable to the Car structure. Write your line of code below and then type it into your program file.

   _____

2. Add the pointer variable to the fastCar structure. Assign to it the address value of the speed variable from slowCar. Write your code below and then add it to your program file.

   _____

3. Enter an output line that will use the pointer variable from fastCar to display a safe driving message. The message should say something similar to, "Everyone should drive at a safe speed like the slow car. The slow car only drives at X miles per hour!" Write your code below and then add it to your program file.

   _____

   _____

   _____

   _____

Step 3: Save Your Program

When you have completed typing the code, save your program once more before moving on to the next step.

Step 4: Build, Link, Run

Enter the commands necessary to build, link, and run your program. If errors occur during any of these processes, check your code, correct any errors, and rerun the program.

Remember to save your program any time you make changes!

Your program should now display an additional safety message. The important feature is not the message, but the fact that you had one structure pointing to another of the same type. Remember, this will help create a linked data structure.

Step 5: Check Your Code

If you have experienced some difficulty in designing and coding your program, or if you are simply curious to see how someone else may have coded the program, then review the sample code below.

```cpp
// Project 8-4.cpp
// Data structure

#include <iostream.h>

struct Car {
    int speed;
    int mpg;
    int fuel;
    int *carPtr;
};

void printLecture(const Car &, int);

main()
{
    int speedLimit;
    int choice;

    Car slowCar;

    slowCar.speed = 35;
    slowCar.mpg = 48;
    slowCar.fuel = 20;

    Car fastCar;

    fastCar.speed = 75;
    fastCar.mpg = 12;
    fastCar.fuel = 20;
    fastCar.carPtr = &slowCar.speed;


    cout << "Enter the speed limit of the road on which you are driving: \n";
    cin >> speedLimit;
```

203

```
      cout << "Are you driving a fast car or a slow car?\n";
      cout << "Enter 1 - Fast Car, or 2 - Slow Car: ";
      cin >> choice;


      if (choice == 1)
         printLecture(fastCar, speedLimit);

      else if (choice == 2)
         printLecture(slowCar, speedLimit);

      cout << "\nEveryone should drive safe like the slow car!";
      cout << "\nThe slow car only drives " << *fastCar.carPtr
           << " miles per hour!\n";

      return 0;
   }

   void printLecture(const Car &c, int sl)
   {
      if (sl < c.speed){
         cout << "You were speeding! You must drive slower!\n";
         cout << "You were driving " << c.speed - sl
              << " MPH over the speed limit!\n";
         cout << "Do you know that you will ONLY get "
              << c.mpg << " MPG at your speed?\n";
         cout << "If you have a " << c.fuel << " gallon gas tank "
              << "then you will only get " << c.mpg * c.fuel
              << " total miles!\n";
         cout << "Slow down!\n";
      }
      else if (sl >= c.speed){
         cout << "You drive as required by the law!\n";
         cout << "You will get better gas mileage that way!\n";
         cout << "With a " << c.fuel << " gallon gas tank "
              << "you should get approximately " << c.mpg * c.fuel
              << " total miles.\n";
         cout << "Good job!!\n";
      }
   }
```

Blocks of the code are pulled out in the following questions. If you coded your own modifications, then explain your equivalent changes in the same places provided below.

1. Explain the following declaration.

```
int *carPtr;
```

_____

2. What is the purpose of the following declaration?

```
fastCar.carPtr = &slowCar.speed;
```

_____

_____

204

3. Explain the following line of code.

```
cout << "\nEveryone should drive safe like the slow car!";
cout << "\nThe slow car only drives " << *fastCar.carPtr
    << " miles per hour!\n";
```

_____

_____

When you're finished, compare your answers with those of your teacher and classmates. Keep working on your ability to analyze C++ code.

PROJECT 8 - 5 : Classes　　Ⓑ

The last project in this lesson is on classes. Structures are the C-style data structure. In C++, structures evolve into classes. Classes enable programmers to create objects that have **attributes**. These attributes are the same data members used in structures; however, with classes, you can add **member functions** or **methods**. As you will see, classes enhance structures.

In this project, you will convert your Car structure into a class. Actually, you'll be redefining the structure as a class.

Step 1: Start Your Compiler

If your compiler is not already running, start it now.

Step 2: Type in Your Code

Type in the code as shown below. Save this program as **Project 8-5.cpp**. _Remember:_ Save often as you type in the code. Add comments to your code as your enter it.

```cpp
// Project 8-5.cpp
// Car Class

#include <iostream.h>

class Car {
public:
    Car();
    void setCar();
    void printCar();

private:
    int speed;
    int mpg;
    int fuel;
};


Car::Car() {speed = mpg = fuel = 0;}

void Car::setCar()
```

```
{
    int s, m, f;

    cout << "How fast can your car go?";
    cout << "\nEnter the speed: ";
    cin >> s;

    cout << "\nHow many miles per gallon does your car get?";
    cout << "\nEnter the miles per gallon: ";
    cin >> m;

    cout << "\nHow much fuel does your car have?";
    cout << "\nEnter the number of gallons in your tank: ";
    cin >> f;

    speed = s;
    mpg = m;
    fuel = f;
}


void Car::printCar()
{
    cout << "\nThe speed of your car is " << speed << ".";
    cout << "\nThe miles per gallon that your car gets is " << mpg << ".";
    cout << "\nThe amount of fuel in your tank is " << fuel << " gallons.";
    cout << "\nAnd you should be able to drive " << fuel * mpg << " miles!\n";
}


main()
{
    Car used;

    used.setCar();
    used.printCar();

    return 0;
}
```

Step 3: Save Your Program

When you have completed typing the code, save your program once more before moving on to the next step.

Step 4: Build, Link, Run

Enter the commands necessary to build, link, and run your program. If errors occur during any of these processes, check your code, correct any errors, and rerun the program.

Remember to save your program any time you make changes!

Step 5: Explain Your Program

1. In the space below, explain the purpose of the *class* keyword and what it accomplishes on this line of code.

```
class Car {
```

_____

_____

The class keyword defines a class type. Once the class is **defined**, the class name can be used to actually create objects of this class.

2. Explain the *public* and *private* labels used within the class.

_____

_____

_____

3. Explain the following private and public members of this class.

```
public:
   Car();
   void setCar();
   void printCar();

private:
   int speed;
   int mpg;
   int fuel;
};
```

_____

_____

_____

_____

_____

4. The following line of code is a constructor member of the class. What is its purpose?

```
Car::Car() {speed = mpg = fuel = 0;}
```

_____

_____

5. Explain the following function. Include an explanation of the header of the function.

```
void Car::setCar()
{
   int s, m, f;

   cout << "How fast can your car go?";
   cout << "\nEnter the speed: ";
   cin >> s;
```

```
    cout << "\nHow many miles per gallon does your car get?";
    cout << "\nEnter the miles per gallon: ";
    cin >> m;

    cout << "\nHow much fuel does your car have?";
    cout << "\nEnter the number of gallons in your tank: ";
    cin >> f;

    speed = s;
    mpg = m;
    fuel = f;
}
```

_____

_____

_____

_____

_____

6. Explain the major differences between the setCar and printCar methods.

```
void Car::printCar()
{
    cout << "\nThe speed of your car is " << speed << ".";
    cout << "\nThe miles per gallon that your car gets is " << mpg << ".";
    cout << "\nThe amount of fuel in your tank is " << fuel << " gallons.";
    cout << "\nAnd you should be able to drive " << fuel * mpg << "
miles!\n";
}
```

_____

_____

_____

7. Following is the main function. Explain it in the space below.

```
main()
{
    Car used;

    used.setCar();
    used.printCar();

    return 0;
}
```

_____

_____

_____

_____

Summary

In this lesson, you created an array that used a double subscript. This, in turn, generates a typical spreadsheet/database table structure with rows and columns.

You learned about data structures and how they let you bundle various data types into a combo package. This means that you can create data structures that actually mean something! You learned that data structures do not need to contain the same data types; you can create structures that are defined specially by you. You also learned that structures could not contain an instance of themselves. However, they can contain pointers to other structures of the same type. These pointers allow you to create linked relationships between structures.

Finally, you explored the class, which is the basis for object-oriented programming. The major difference between classes and structures is that classes are objects that have attributes. You learned how to move data types into the class (data members), and move functions in as member functions. This lets you control all features of the class. You will learn more about classes in the next lesson.

LESSON 8 REVIEW QUESTIONS

SHORT ANSWER

Define the following in the space provided.

1. Arrays

2. Pointer

3. Declare

4. Single subscript array

5. Multiple subscript array

6. Subscripts

7. Structures

8. Struct

9. Aggregate data type

_____

_____

10. class

_____

_____

11. User-defined type

_____

_____

_____

12. Object

_____

13. Initialize

_____

14. Constant variable

_____

15. Structure members

_____

16. Instance

_____

17. Linking

_____

_____

18. Passing by reference

_____

_____

19. Dot operator

_____

20. Member access operator

_____

21. Binary scope resolution operator

_____

_____

22. Class name

_____

23. Methods

_____

24. Member functions

_____

25. Data members

_____

26. Member access specifiers

_____

_____

27. Public members

_____

28. Private members

_____

_____

29. Constructor

_____

WRITTEN QUESTIONS

Write your answers to the following questions in the space provided.

1. What is the difference between a single subscript array and a multiple subscript array?

_____

_____

2. What is the maximum number of array subscripts in C++?

_____

3. When would a double, or other multiple, subscript array prove to be useful?

_____

4. Explain the benefits of creating a data structure.

_____

_____

5. Explain the differences between a structure and a class.

_____

6. Design a structure that contains three data members.

_____

_____

_____

_____

_____

7. Design a class that contains a constructor and one other public method, plus the three data members from the structure in #6.

_____

_____

_____

_____

_____

8. Explain the benefits of using classes.

_____

_____

_____

TESTING YOUR SKILLS

⏱ **Estimated Time:**
Application 8-1 1 hour
Application 8-2 1 hour
Application 8-3 30 minutes

APPLICATION 8-1

1. Split the code in *Project 8-2* into two separate functions. Move the function prototypes into a header file. Save the code in a file named **App8-1.cpp**. Name the header file **Lesson8.h**.

APPLICATION 8-2

1. Create a user interface (simple prompts will do), that collects data from the user. Use *Project 8-3.cpp* as the basis for the interface. Save your modified code as **App8-2.cpp**. The data you are seeking from the user is the information needed for the variables in *both* the slow car and the fast car.

APPLICATION 8-3

1. Create a new car instance in the same class you created in *Project 8-5*. Simply modify the code from *Project 8-5.cpp*, and name the modified file **App8-3.cpp**. (*Hint:* You simply need to add code to the main function.)

CRITICAL THINKING

⏱ **Estimated Time: 6–8 hours**

SCANS

Create a multiple string array that will "hold" the values of a deck of cards. One portion of the array will hold the suits—hearts, diamonds, clubs, and spades. The other part of the array will hold the face—ace down to the number 2.

Once you have the array created, shuffle the array, and then deal the cards.

This project will require you to use all your C++ skills and knowledge. Good luck!

CLASSES—OBJECT-ORIENTED PROGRAMMING

Introduction

Lesson 8 ended by showing you how to create a simple class from a structure. In Project 8-5, you were introduced to some of the features of classes. This lesson begins with a more in-depth discussion of classes.

Structures, the C *aggregate data type*, make the evolution to classes easy. Structures, if you will remember, are basically collections of data types. They are a user-created type that does not need to consist of the same data type.

A class is also a *user-defined type*. However, a class contains functions as well as data. So now you have data, and things you can do with the data, all stored in the same place. The class is now referred to as an *object*, and it forms the unit of programming in C++. This forms the basis of *object-oriented programming*. Think about the implications—data and related functions that form a complete unit.

You will also see that you can protect data from the user by limiting access to it. This is known as separating the *interface* from the *implementation*. In simpler terms, this means that the user can execute the program without knowing the details of how it actually runs. And isn't this the way all the programs you use work?

Shift back to user-defined type for a moment. The user can define classes, like structures. You create the data types that they need to work with. Plus, there are multitudes of classes available from various sources that you can also expand upon or modify. As you will see, C++ is quite an explosive language!

This lesson will focus on the following:

■ **Designing and defining a class.** This will be a continuation of the last project you worked on in Lesson 8. You will start by creating another class similar to the one you created in that project, and then you will explore other class topics.

- **Creating classes and class members.** Since you define the class, you will decide what the class will look like, what it will include, and what it will do. You'll begin to understand the proper way to keep data away from the user.

- **Separating interface from implementation.** One of the major advantages of classes is that they provide you with a mechanism for protecting code from the user. You, as the programmer, decide how the user will gain access to the data. This is known as separating the interface (how the user uses the program) from the implementation (how the program works "under the hood").

- **Accessing class members and controlling access to class members.** If you are going to separate interface from implementation, then you need to provide users with a way to manipulate the data. These methods will also control what can be done with the data.

- **Deriving a class.** Classes can be reused. After all, that's the beauty of object-oriented programming. Users can start with an existing class and *inherit* the set of properties into a new class. This is known as *inheritance*. You start with a *base class* and *derive* a new class from an old one, while retaining the properties of the old one. Why reinvent the wheel?

PROJECT 9-1 : A Simple Class

You will begin this lesson with the creation of a class. You will be provided with the information needed to define the class. If you are unsure of the details regarding the creation of a class, review your Project 8-5 notes.

In this project, you will be creating a class that will create a dog—your dog. You will be using this class in the first few lesson projects.

Step 1: Start Your Compiler

Start your compiler if it is not already running.

Step 2: Design Your Class

You will be creating a Pet class called "dog." It could be any dog, so when you create your dog think of the attributes that a dog may have.

1. Create your Pet class definition by writing it first in the space below. Your class will be called Pet. Your data members will be those attributes that your dog-type Pet possesses, such as weight, color, breed, sounds, etc. You also need to create member functions (methods). What does your dog do? You will not need to create the method prototypes right away, but you should be able to define your data types.

    Your dog is a brown mutt and weighs 45 pounds. The dog makes the "arf" sound. It will "speak" when asked and it will tell you about itself if asked.

    _____

    _____

    _____

    _____

    _____

    _____

    _____

2. In the space below, create a flowchart, narrative, or other explanation of how your functions will work alone, and then together. For example, your dog speaks when asked, and will tell you about itself when asked. You will need at least these two functions, both being related because they both involve "speaking." Plus, you may need additional functions.

_____
_____
_____
_____
_____
_____
_____
_____
_____
_____
_____
_____
_____
_____

3. Using the information you created in step 2, lay out your member function prototypes and definitions in the space below.

_____
_____
_____
_____
_____
_____
_____
_____
_____
_____
_____
_____
_____
_____
_____
_____
_____

_____
_____
_____
_____
_____
_____
_____
_____
_____
_____
_____
_____
_____
_____
_____
_____

4. At this point you should have your class definition ready to go. You should have your data members and all of your functions. Did you remember to create a constructor that will initialize all your data variables to a consistent state? Remember, you should create at least one default constructor to initialize data members. If you have not created one, create your constructor on the lines below.

_____
_____
_____

Make sure that your data members are labeled as private and that your member functions are labeled as public. This will help protect data from being accessed directly by users.

5. Lay out your main function in the space below. Insert comments in the appropriate places.

_____
_____
_____
_____
_____
_____
_____
_____
_____

6. Organize your blocks of code in the space below.

_____

_____

_____

_____

_____

_____

_____

_____

_____

_____

Step 3: Type in Your Code

Type your code in as you've written it above. Save the file as **Project 9-1.cpp**.

Step 4: Save Your Program

Once you have finished typing in your code, save your code one final time before compiling your program.

Step 5: Build, Link, Run

Enter the commands necessary to build, link, and run your program. If errors occur during any of these processes, check your code, correct any errors, and rerun the program.

Your program should perform the tasks listed in step 1. If your program performs those tasks, then it works properly.

Step 6: Review Your Code

Now that your program has run successfully, answer the following questions. Review your answers with your classmates and teacher.

1. How many header files did you need to use for your program to compile properly? List the header files you needed to use.

_____

_____

_____

_____

_____

_____

_____

_____

2. Explain the data members used to "define" your dog.

_____

_____

_____

_____

_____

_____

_____

3. Explain each of your four member functions—both the prototypes and the definitions.

_____

_____

_____

_____

_____

_____

_____

4. Explain each of the data types declared in the main().

_____

_____

_____

_____

_____

_____

_____

_____

5. Explain why you have separate data types declared in main.

_____

_____

6. Explain why each member function used in main() is preceded by a dot member operator.

_____

7. Explain your input sequence, if separate from your member functions.

_____

_____

_____

_____

_____

_____

8. Explain your output sequence, if separate from your member functions.

_____

_____

_____

_____

_____

_____

_____

_____

Step 7: Check Your Code

The code below is just one example of creating a "dog." If your code is different and it works—that's great! Not everyone programs the same.

```cpp
// Project 9-1.cpp
// Pet class

#include <iostream.h>
#include <string.h>

class Pet {
    public:
        Pet();
        void setPet(int w, char b[], char c[], char s[]);
        void printPet();
        void speakPet();

    private:
        int weight;
        char breed[20];
        char color[10];
        char sound[10];
};

Pet::Pet()
{
    weight = 0;
    strcpy(breed, "");
    strcpy(color, "");
    strcpy(sound, "");
}

void Pet::setPet(int w, char b[], char c[], char s[])
{
    weight = w;
    strcpy(breed, b);
    strcpy(color, c);
    strcpy(sound, s);
}

void Pet::printPet()
```

```cpp
{
    cout << "\nMy dog is a " << breed << "!\n";
    cout << "He weighs " << weight << " pounds and is " << color
        << " in color.\n";
    cout << "I love my dog!! \n\n";
}

void Pet::speakPet()
{
    cout << "\n\n" << sound << "\n\n";
}



main()
{
    Pet dog;
    int choice;
    int w;
    char b[20];
    char c[10];
    char s[10];

    cout << "Please enter the breed of your dog. ";
    cin >> b;

    cout << "\nPlease enter the color of your dog. ";
    cin >> c;

    cout << "\nPlease enter the sound your dog makes. ";
    cin >> s;

    cout << "\nPlease enter the weight of your dog. ";
    cin >> w;

    dog.setPet( w,  b,  c,  s);


    while(1) {
        cout << "\n\nMy dog would like to speak with you! ";
        cout << "\n1) Speak, Dog, Speak";
        cout << "\n2) Personal statistics";
        cout << "\n3) Exit\n";
        cout << "\nEnter your choice: ";
        cin >> choice;

        if (choice == 1)
            dog.speakPet();
        else if (choice == 2)
            dog.printPet();
        else if (choice == 3)
            break;
    }

    return 0;
}
```

Now you have a dog that you can change without a great deal of effort, and you don't need to clean up after it either!

PROJECT 9-2:
An Enhanced Dog—Constructors & Destructors

In this project, you will "enhance" your dog. Since a new concept will be introduced in this project, the code for you to input will be provided. It will be your responsibility to research the code and explain what it does.

As you have learned, the purpose of a constructor is to initialize your private data members. In this project, you will use a constructor to call a function that requests input from the user. By doing this, you will be initializing private data members as the user inputs the information needed. This method also eliminates the need to "pass" information from public variables to private variables, and still use *encapsulation*.

You will also call a *destructor*. The purpose of the destructor is to signal the compiler that memory can be freed. Remember that the destructor is called automatically. However, if you want to see the destructor work, or you want something to happen when it is called, then you can create your own destructor. In this project, you will incorporate a goodbye message as part of the destructor.

Feel free to enhance your dog beyond what's shown in the instruction.

Step 1: Start Your Compiler

Start your compiler if it is not already running.

Step 2: Type in Your Code

Type in your code as follows. Save the file as **Project 9-2.cpp**.

```
//Project 9-2.cpp
//Programmer: Mahsa Anvarinia
//Pet class

#include <iostream.h>
#include <string.h>


class Pet {
public:
   Pet();
   ~Pet();
   void getInfo();
   void makeSound();
   void printInfo();

private:
   float size;
   char color[15];
   char breed[50];
```

221

```cpp
      char sound[10];
};

Pet::Pet()
{ getInfo(); }

Pet::~Pet()
{ cout << "(^_~) Bye Bye!!! " << endl; }

void Pet::getInfo()
{
    cout << "Please input the breed: ";
    cin >> breed;

    cout << "Please input the color: ";
    cin >> color;

    cout << "Please input the size: ";
    cin >> size;

    strcpy(sound, "Arf!");
}

void Pet::makeSound()
{
    cout << sound << endl;
}


void Pet::printInfo()
{
    cout << "Hi! I am a " << color << " " << breed << ".\n";
    cout << "And I weigh " << size << " pounds!" << endl;
}


//non member functions
char menu();
void hitEnter();


main()
{
    Pet dog;
    char choice = '0';


    choice = menu();
    while (choice != '3')
    {
        if (choice == '1')
```

```
                        dog.makeSound();

             else if (choice == '2')
                     dog.printInfo();

             hitEnter();

             choice = menu();
      }

      return 0;

}


char menu()
{
   char x = '0';

   while ((x != '1') && (x != '2') && (x !='3'))
   {
        cout << endl;
        cout << "1. Speak" << endl;
        cout << "2. Ask"   << endl;
        cout << "3. Exit"  << endl;
        cout << endl << "Please enter a choice ( 1-3 ): ";
        cin >> x;
   }

   return x;
}


void hitEnter()
{
   char junk = ' ';
   char go = ' ';

   junk = cin.get();

   while (go != 10)
   {
        cout << "Hit <enter> to continue...";
        go = cin.get();
   }
}
```

Step 3: Save Your Program

Once you have finished typing in your code, save your code one final time before compiling your program.

Step 4: Build, Link, Run

Enter the commands necessary to build, link, and run your program. If errors occur during any of these processes, check your code, correct any errors, and rerun the program.

Make sure you test your program. This project should execute in a similar manner to Project 9-1. However, you will notice that the code is different. Remember—everyone programs the same solution differently!

Step 5: Review Your Code

Now that your program has run successfully, review your code so that you understand the enhancements used in this project.

The code above is just one example of an enhanced dog (as coded by Mahsa Anvarinia). Mahsa has added some features that prove to be very useful—and she enhances the concept of separating interface from implementation!

1. The constructor from Project 9-2 is shown below. Explain it in the space following it.

```
Pet::Pet()
{ getInfo(); }
```

_____

_____

2. When is the constructor performed? Look in the main function.

_____

3. How does this method of initializing private data members enforce the separation of interface and implementation?

_____

_____

_____

4. How does this method of initializing members eliminate the need for public variables in main?

_____

_____

_____

5. Explain the destructor from the sample Project 9-2 code.

```
Pet::-Pet()
{ cout << "(^_-) Bye Bye!!! " << endl; }
```

_____

_____

_____

6. When is the destructor called?

_____

_____

224

LESSON 9

Copying/scanning is not permitted and may be a violation of copyright laws.
© 2000 by South-Western Educational Publishing.

Your program probably looks different from Project 9-1. But if it works, it doesn't matter! You now have an idea of the power of constructors and destructors.

P R O J E C T   9 - 3 : Inheritance—Derived Classes ①

This project deals with inheritance. Even though you won't get any money from a rich relative, you will receive access to a rich set of functions that will make your programs dynamic!

In Project 9-1, you created a single, simple class. In this project, you will create a base class and then derive a specific class from the base. Instead of having a Pet class and then creating an instance of Pet called dog, you will have a Pet class that "spins off" a Dog class and then create an instance of Dog.

A base class is usually a generic class from which the derived class can inherit attributes and methods. You then create instances of the derived class. However, you can still access all the public members in the base class through the public methods of the Dog class. The theory is that everything in the base class is generic. For example, all pets have an owner, have a color, have a type (dog, cat, bird, etc.). Then, the specific types (dog, cat, bird, etc.) have additional attributes that only they possess. For example, cats chase mice, dogs eat bones, etc. The attributes in the derived class become enhanced.

You will modify your code from Project 9-1 into classes.

Step 1: Start Your Compiler

Start your compiler if it is not already running.

Step 2: Modify Your Code

Modify your code from **Project 9-1.cpp** exactly as shown below. Save this program as **Project 9-3.cpp**.

```
// Project 9-3.cpp
// Base class/Derived class

#include <iostream.h>
#include <string.h>

class Pet {
    public:
        Pet();
        void setPet();
        void printPet();
        virtual void speakPet();

    private:
        int weight;
        char owner[10];
        char species[10];
        char color[10];
        char sound[10];
};
```

2 2 5

```
class Dog : public Pet {
   public:
        Dog();
        void setPet();
        void printPet();
        virtual void speakPet();

   private:
        int bones;
        char breed[10];
        char typeCoat[10];
};

Pet::Pet()
{
   setPet();
}

void Pet::setPet()
{
   cout << "Who owns this pet (first name)? ";
   cin >> owner;

   cout << "\nPlease enter the species of your pet. ";
   cin >> species;

   cout << "\nPlease enter the color of your pet. ";
   cin >> color;

   cout << "\nPlease enter the sound your dog makes. ";
   cin >> sound;

   cout << "\nPlease enter the weight of your dog. ";
   cin >> weight;
}

void Pet::printPet()
{
   cout << "\n" << owner << "'s pet is a " << species << "!\n";
   cout << "He weighs " << weight << " pounds and is " << color
        << " in color.\n";
   cout << "I love my " << species << "!\n\n";
}

void Pet::speakPet()
{
   cout << "\n\n" << sound << "\n\n";
}


Dog::Dog()
   :Pet()
{
   setPet();
```

```
}

void Dog::setPet()
{
   cout << "\nPlease enter the breed of your dog. ";
   cin >> breed;

   cout << "\nPlease enter the type coat your dog has. ";
   cin >> typeCoat;

   cout << "\nPlease enter the number of bones your dog eats. ";
   cin >> bones;
}


void Dog::printPet()
{
   Pet::printPet();
   cout << "\nOh, by the way! My dog is a " << breed << ".";
   cout << "\nAnd he has a " << typeCoat << " coat!";
   cout << "\nPlus, he doesn't know that I know - "
        << "but he's buried " << bones << " bones!";
}


void Dog::speakPet()
{
   Pet::speakPet();
}


main()
{
   Dog dog;
   int choice;

   while(1) {
        cout << "\n\nMy dog would like to speak with you! ";
        cout << "\n1) Speak, Dog, Speak";
        cout << "\n2) Personal statistics";
        cout << "\n3) Exit\n";
        cout << "\nEnter your choice: ";
        cin >> choice;

        if (choice == 1)
           dog.speakPet();
        else if (choice == 2)
           dog.printPet();
        else if (choice == 3)
           break;
   }

   return 0;
}
```

Step 4: Save Your Program

Once you have finished typing in your code, save your code one final time before compiling your program.

Step 5: Build, Link and Run

Enter the commands necessary to build and link your program. If errors occur during any of these processes, check your code, correct any errors, and relink the program.

Your new program should be an enhanced version of Project 9-1.

Step 6: Review Your Code

Now that your program has run successfully, review your code with your classmates and teacher.

1. In the space below, explain the following block of code.

```
class Pet {
    public:
        Pet();
        void setPet();
        void printPet();
        virtual void speakPet();

    private:
        int weight;
        char owner[10];
        char species[10];
        char color[10];
        char sound[10];
};
```

_____

_____

_____

_____

2. What is the purpose of the following block of code?

```
class Dog : public Pet {
    public:
        Dog();
        void setPet();
        void printPet();
        virtual void speakPet();

    private:
        int bones;
        char breed[10];
        char typeCoat[10];
};
```

_____

_____

3. Explain the following block of code.

```
Dog::Dog()
   :Pet()
{
   setPet();
}
```

_____

_____

4. Explain the functions that execute when the following line of code is performed.

```
Dog dog;
```

_____

_____

_____

_____

_____

5. Explain the execution of the following if/else structure.

```
    if (choice == 1)
        dog.speakPet();
    else if (choice == 2)
        dog.printPet();
    else if (choice == 3)
        break;
}
```

_____

_____

_____

_____

_____

When the derived class inherits functions from the base class, you can use the functions as they are, or you can override them. Overriding lets you use a function with the same name and have it execute differently than the original. All functions from Pet are overloaded with the exception of speakPet().

6. Explain the following overridden function.

```
void Dog::printPet()
{
   Pet::printPet();
```

```
    cout << "\nOh, by the way! My dog is a " << breed << ".";
    cout << "\nAnd he has a " << typeCoat << " coat!";
    cout << "\nPlus, he doesn't know that I know - "
        << "but he's buried " << bones << " bones!";
}
```

7. Explain why the following function calls a function from the base class.

```
void Dog::speakPet()
{
    Pet::speakPet();
}
```

_____

_____

_____

The benefit of using base and derived classes will become more apparent as you derive more and more classes off the base class.

PROJECT 9 - 4 : Virtual Functions

Virtual functions represent another benefit of base and derived classes. In the last project you might have noticed that you accessed the Dog class directly by using the instance name in conjunction with the dot member operator. In this project, you will see how you can dynamically access a function by making it virtual.

A virtual function is one that is declared with the _virtual_ keyword. Once a function is declared virtual, it is virtual in every class that inherits it. For clarity, the virtual keyword should be used in declaring the function in every derived class.

A virtual function is one that you can access through a ***base class pointer*** or ***reference***. Once you reference the base class function, it digs its way through the base class and each derived class until it finds the proper function to execute. However, this will not work unless the function in the base class is declared virtual.

Step 1: Start Your Compiler

If your compiler is not already running, start it now.

Step 2: Modify Your Code

Open your **Project 9-3.cpp** file. Modify your code as directed below. Save the program as **Project 9-4.cpp**. _Remember:_ Save often as you type in the code. Add comments to your code as you enter it.

```cpp
// Project 9-4.cpp
// Base class/Derived class with virtual function

#include <iostream.h>
#include <string.h>

class Pet {
    public:
        Pet();
        void setPet();
        void printPet();
        virtual void speakPet() const;

    private:
        int weight;
        char owner[10];
        char species[10];
        char color[10];
        char sound[10];
};

class Dog : public Pet {
    public:
        Dog();
        void setPet();
        void printPet();
        virtual void speakPet() const;

    private:
        int bones;
        char breed[10];
        char typeCoat[10];
};

Pet::Pet()
{
    setPet();
}

void Pet::setPet()
{
    cout << "Who owns this pet (first name)? ";
    cin >> owner;

    cout << "\nPlease enter the species of your pet. ";
    cin >> species;

    cout << "\nPlease enter the color of your pet. ";
    cin >> color;

    cout << "\nPlease enter the sound your dog makes. ";
    cin >> sound;
```

```cpp
    cout << "\nPlease enter the weight of your dog. ";
    cin >> weight;
}

void Pet::printPet()
{
    cout << "\n" << owner << "'s pet is a " << species << "!\n";
    cout << "He weighs " << weight << " pounds and is " << color
         << " in color.\n";
    cout << "I love my " << species << "!\n\n";
}

void Pet::speakPet() const
{
    cout << "\n\n" << sound << "\n\n";
}


Dog::Dog()
   :Pet()
{
    setPet();
}


void Dog::setPet()
{
    cout << "\nPlease enter the breed of your dog. ";
    cin >> breed;

    cout << "\nPlease enter the type coat your dog has. ";
    cin >> typeCoat;

    cout << "\nPlease enter the number of bones your dog eats. ";
    cin >> bones;
}


void Dog::printPet()
{
    Pet::printPet();
    cout << "\nOh, by the way! My dog is a " << breed << ".";
    cout << "\nAnd he has a " << typeCoat << " coat!";
    cout << "\nPlus, he doesn't know that I know - "
         << "but he's buried " << bones << " bones!";
}


void Dog::speakPet() const
{
    Pet::speakPet();
}
```

```
void virtualSpeakRef(const Pet &);

main()
{
    Dog dog;
    int choice;

    while(1) {
        cout << "\n\nMy dog would like to speak with you! ";
        cout << "\n1) Speak, Dog, Speak";
        cout << "\n2) Personal statistics";
        cout << "\n3) Exit\n";
        cout << "\nEnter your choice: ";
        cin >> choice;

        if (choice == 1)
                virtualSpeakRef(dog);
        else if (choice == 2)
                dog.printPet();
        else if (choice == 3)
                break;
    }

    return 0;
}

void virtualSpeakRef(const Pet &baseClassRef)
{

    baseClassRef.speakPet();

}
```

Step 3: Save Your Program

When you have completed typing the code, save your program once more before moving on to the next step.

Step 4: Build, Link, Run

Enter the commands necessary to build, link, and run your program. If errors occur during any of these processes, check your code, correct any errors, and rerun the program.

Remember to save your program any time you make changes!

Your program should *not* visibly work any differently. Any changes made because of the virtual functions will work behind the scenes. If your program works after you made the changes, then the virtual function is working. If it does not work, then the changes you made are incorrect.

Step 5: Explain Your Code

The only difference in this program is the use of virtual functions. Therefore, concentrate on those lines of code.

1. Explain the following line of code.

```
virtual void speakPet() const;
```

_____

_____

2. Explain the following line of code.

```
void virtualSpeakRef(const Pet &);
```

_____

_____

_____

_____

_____

_____

3. Explain the following line of code.

```
if (choice == 1)
    virtualSpeakRef(dog);
```

_____

_____

4. Explain the following block of code.

```
void virtualSpeakRef(const Pet &baseClassRef)
{

    baseClassRef.speakPet();

}
```

_____

_____

_____

_____

   When you're finished, compare your answers with those of your teacher and classmates. Keep working on your ability to analyze C++ code. You should now have a pretty good overview of classes.

PROJECT 9-5 : Multiple Instances of a Class

This project uses many of the features you've worked with throughout this book. You'll start by defining a simple employee class in terms of members, but the members themselves prove to be slightly difficult to work with. You will use arrays, pointers, functions, for loops, and multiple class instances in order to input multiple employees.

234

Step 1: Start Your Compiler

Start your compiler if it is not already running.

Step 2: Design Your Class

You will create an Employee class that contains data members for first name, last name, and E-mail address. You will need to input the information and print it. Use the questions below as a guide to laying out and coding your program.

1. In the space below, lay out your class definition. You have enough information to name your class and to create your data members. You will need to use character or string arrays. You also know that you need three member functions (methods). You will not need to create the method prototypes right away, but you should be able to define your data types.

    _____
    _____
    _____
    _____
    _____
    _____
    _____

2. Create a flowchart, narrative, or other explanation of how your functions will work together. You will be inputting information and then displaying it. So, you will need to gather information from the user and then manipulate it in order to display it to the monitor. You will need to separate the interface (user interactivity) from the implementation (how the program works).

    _____
    _____
    _____
    _____
    _____
    _____
    _____
    _____
    _____
    _____
    _____
    _____
    _____

3. Lay out your member function prototypes and definitions.

    _____
    _____

4. Lay out your main function. Insert comments in the appropriate places.

5. Organize your blocks of code in the space below.

_____

_____

_____

_____

_____

_____

_____

_____

_____

_____

_____

_____

_____

_____

Step 3: Type in Your Code

Type your code in as you've written it above. Save the file as **Project 9-5.cpp**.

Step 4: Save Your Program

Once you have finished typing in your code, save your code one final time before compiling your program.

Step 5: Build, Link, Run

Enter the commands necessary to build, link, and run your program. If errors occur during any of these processes, check your code, correct any errors, and rerun the program.

Your program should ask you for a specific number of employee names and E-mail addresses, and then print them out when finished. If your program does this, then it works properly.

Step 6: Review Your Code

Now that your program has run successfully, answer the following questions. Review your answers with your classmates and teacher.

1. How many header files did you need to use for your program to compile properly? List the header files you needed to use.

_____

_____

_____

_____

_____

_____

_____

2. Explain the data member used to store your character data members.

_____

_____

_____

_____

_____

_____

_____

3. Explain each of your three member functions—both the prototypes and the definitions.

_____

_____

_____

_____

_____

_____

_____

_____

4. Explain each of the data types declared in the main().

_____

_____

_____

_____

_____

_____

_____

5. Explain why each member function used in main() is preceded by a dot member operator.

_____

_____

6. Explain your input sequence.

_____

_____

_____

_____

7. Explain your output sequence.

Step 7: Check Your Code

Below is a sample of this program (as coded by Tom Roncevic and modified by John Sestak). You can use this example as an alternative to your code.

```
// Project 9-5.cpp
// Simple Employee Class
// Programmer: Tom Roncevic modified by John Sestak

#include <iostream.h>
#include <string.h>

class Person
{
private:
    char fname[20];
    char lname[20];
    char email[30];


public:
    Person();
    void setadd (char *first, char *last, char *add, Person *ptr);
    void displayadd (Person *ptr);
};


Person::Person()
{
    char fname[20] = "";
    char lname[20] = "";
    char email[30] = "";
}
```

```cpp
void Person::setadd(char *first, char *last, char *add, Person *ptr)
{
    strcpy (ptr->fname, first);
    strcpy (ptr->lname, last);
    strcpy (ptr->email, add);
}


void Person::displayadd(Person *ptr)
{
    cout << ptr << "\t";
    cout << ptr->fname << " ";
    cout << ptr->lname << " ";
    cout << ptr->email << endl;
}


main()
{
    Person p;
    Person csp[11];
    unsigned num;
    char firstname[20];
    char lastname[20];
    char emailaddress[30];

    for (num = 1; num <= 10; num++)
    {
        cout << "Person #" << num << endl;
        cout << "Enter the person's first name: ";
        cin >> firstname;

        cout << "Enter the person's last name: ";
        cin >> lastname;

        cout << "Enter the person's email address: ";
        cin >> emailaddress;

        p.setadd(firstname, lastname, emailaddress, &csp[num]);
    }

    for (num = 1; num <= 10; num++)
    {
        if (num < 10)
            cout << " " << num << ". ";
        else
            cout << num << ". ";
        p.displayadd(&csp[num]);
        cout << endl;
    }

    return 0;
}
```

You will notice that memory addresses are added to the output. To make sure the pointer was working properly, the value of the pointer for each array entry was printed so that you could see the memory addresses. This code would be removed before the program was used.

Summary

Classes are powerful objects. You can now define data types that you need for your programs. You are no longer limited to using what is provided to you.

In this lesson, you created a single, simple class. From that single class, you learned how to enhance constructors and destructors. You explored the concept of inheritance. By creating a base class and then deriving a class from the base class, you can create a multitude of objects that can reuse various attributes and methods of classes above it.

By incorporating virtual functions, you can leave it up to the program to find the proper function to use. Classes, as you've probably realized, are an integral part of C++.

Finally, you learned how to create multiple instances of a class. Now, you can have a whole kennel of dogs, or a whole list of employees and E-mail addresses!

LESSON 9 REVIEW QUESTIONS

SHORT ANSWER

Define the following in the space provided.

1. Classes

2. Objects

3. Data types

4. Methods

5. Constructor

6. Destructor

7. Inheritance

_____

_____

8. Base class

_____

9. Derived class

_____

10. User-defined type

_____

11. Virtual function

_____

_____

_____

12. Encapsulation

_____

13. Object-oriented programming

_____

14. Data members

_____

15. Interface

_____

16. Implementation

_____

_____

17. Base class pointer

_____

_____

18. Base class reference

_____

_____

19. Dynamic binding

_____

_____

_____

WRITTEN QUESTIONS

Write your answers to the following questions in the space provided.

1. Define class.

_____

2. Why should data members be defined as private?

_____

_____

3. Why should member functions be public?

_____

_____

4. Explain what is meant by separating interface and implementation.

_____

_____

5. Explain the differences between a base class and a derived class.

_____

_____

_____

6. Explain virtual functions.

_____

_____

_____

7. Explain dynamic binding.

_____

_____

_____

_____

8. Explain the benefits of using classes.

_____

_____

TESTING YOUR SKILLS

⏱ **Estimated Time:**

Application 9-1 3 hours
Application 9-2 3 hours

APPLICATION 9-1

In Project 9-3, you coded a program so that your dog would speak when asked and would tell you about itself. In this application, you're going to add the ability for your dog to ask for food.

The function should work like this: If the dog is hungry, it will search for buried bones. If there are no buried bones, it will bark for you to give it some bones to eat. The dog will eat until filled. If there are any bones left, the dog will bury them. When the dog gets hungry again, it will first "sniff" around for buried bones. If it finds them, it will eat them; if not, the dog will bark for more.

Open the **Project 9-3.cpp** file and save it as **App9-1.cpp**. Add an eating function to the program.

APPLICATION 9-2

This application will expand on Application 9-1. Open your **App9-1.cpp** file and save it as **App9-2.cpp**.

You will add a function that measures how much your dog likes you depending on what you do with it. The dog still does every other function, but now it reacts to you by how you interact with it. You can take it for a walk, you can play catch with it, etc. This will earn you "likeness" points. But if you tug on the dog's leash, or you dig up its bones—watch out!!

From your behavior, the dog will measure how much it likes you!

CRITICAL THINKING

⏱ **Estimated Time: 6–8 hours**

Using all the techniques presented in this lesson, create a virtual zoo. This zoo will be built out of an animal base class (all animals have similar basic traits). Then each animal housed in the zoo will become a derived class. If you have more than one type of animal, then you will have multiple instances. Each specific type of animal will possess traits specific to it and will do things (functions) specific to its type.

You can make this as easy or as complicated as you wish. On the easy end, you can simply create multiple dog-style derived classes. On the complex end, you can have the animals interact with each other. For example, the lion would probably eat the deer!

FILE INPUT AND OUTPUT

OBJECTIVES

Upon completion of this lesson, you should be able to:

- Create a sequential access file.

- Enter data into a sequential access file.

- Read data from a sequential access file.

- Create an empty random access file.

- Enter data into a random access file.

- Read data from a random access file.

⏱ **Estimated Time: 7 hours**

Introduction

Everything you've done so far in this book, and probably in your C++ class, has dealt with input, output, and manipulating data in memory. However, even though most program activity does takes place in memory, users still have a need to store data for later use. This topic is addressed now.

Files are accessed in either a *sequential* manner or in a *random* manner. In most cases today, *random access* is the norm. However, there are some instances where sequential access is still important. Sequential access is a method of storing the data in the order of its *record key field*. Any data added to a sequential file is added to the end, or *appended*. Random access is a method of storing the data in any order. Data is input and stored wherever, but it is still in the file. And the data is accessible directly, without searching all the other records in the file.

File access is not hard. The methods are simple and straightforward. You begin by creating a file, then entering data. From that point forward you can manipulate the files as you see fit. You will be introduced to new keywords and new functions, but they are very similar to objects you've used in other lessons in this book.

This lesson will focus on the following:

- **Creating a sequential access file.** You will create a sequential access file on the same disk that you store your programs.

- **Entering data into a sequential access file.** You will use methods and functions you created in earlier projects in conjunction with new functions to input data into the file. One of the interesting things you will notice is that you will be able to view your data files using a simple word processor like Notepad.

- **Reading data from a sequential access file.** Once you get data into the file, you will be able to access it and display it for users.

- **Creating a random access file.** Unlike a sequential access file, the random access file should be created empty and then the data should be added.

- **Entering data into a random access file.** Data can be added to a random access file in a sequential order or a random order. In this lesson, you'll enter data in a random manner.

- **Reading data from a random access file.** As with the sequential access files, users need to be able to access data from the permanent files and display it to the screen. You will learn how to accomplish that task with the random access file.

PROJECT 10-1:
Create a Sequential Access File

In this project you will be creating a simple sequential access file. Sequential access files are those files stored in the order of their record key field. A *field* is a group of related characters, such as a name. A group of fields forms a *record*. A record is one particular instance of a structure or a class, such as first name, last name, middle initial, etc. A *file* is a collection of related records. However, when dealing with files, the structure or class is referred to as a file. And the files can be collectively grouped into a *database*.

You will create a sequential access file using information collected in Project 9-5. Once you get a handle on creating one sequential access file, you can essentially mimic the method to create multiple files. So, it's time to get started!

Step 1: Start Your Compiler

If your compiler is not already running, start it now.

Step 2: Type in Your Code

Type in your code as follows. Save it with the filename **Project 10-1.cpp**. Make sure you save your file often.

```
// Project 10-1
// Create a sequential access file
// Programmer: <Your Name>

#include <iostream.h>
#include <fstream.h>
#include <stdlib.h>


main()
{
    char fname[20];
```

```
      char lname[20];
      char email[30];

      ofstream outEmailFile ("email.dat", ios::out);

      if (!outEmailFile)
      {
         cerr << "Could not create file!" << "\n";
         exit(1);
      }

      cout << "Enter the first name, last name, and e-mail address "
           << "of your contact:";
      cout << "\nUse end-of-file to terminate input.\nNext entry? ";

      while (cin >> fname >> lname >> email)
      {
         outEmailFile << fname << " " << lname << " " << email << "\n";
         cout << "\nNext entry? ";
      }

      cout << "\n";

      outEmailFile.close();

      return 0;
}
```

Step 3: Save Your Program

Once you have finished typing in your code, save your code one final time before compiling your program.

Step 4: Build, Link, Run

Enter the commands necessary to build, link, and run your program. If errors occur during any of these processes, check your code, correct any errors, and rerun the program.

The program should create a file in your program directory, wherever you store and execute your programs from. The file will be named **email.dat**. This file will store the information that the user inputs in the format provided. Basically, the file will be in text format.

The user will be prompted to input first name, last name, and E-mail addresses. When the data is input, the user will notify the program by using the end-of-file input keystrokes.

If you want to see the data stored in this file before you read it in the next project, then open the file with Notepad or another text editor. If you decide to run this program multiple times you will always have only one file. Each time this program is executed it overwrites the existing file—so be careful!

Step 5: Review Your Code

Now that your program has run successfully, answer the following questions. Review your answers with your classmates and teacher.

1. How many header files did you need to use for your program to compile properly? List the header files you needed to use.

2. Explain why each of the above header files needed to be included.

_____

_____

3. Explain the following line of code.

```
ofstream outEmailFile ("email.dat", ios::out);
```

_____

_____

_____

4. Explain the following block of code.

```
if (!outEmailFile)
{
   cerr << "Could not create file!" << "\n";
   exit(1);
}
```

_____

_____

5. Explain the following block of code.

```
while (cin >> fname >> lname >> email)
{
   outEmailFile << fname << " " << lname << " " << email << "\n";
   cout << "\nNext entry? ";
}
```

_____

_____

_____

_____

_____

6. Explain the following line of code. Explain why it is, or is not, necessary for this line of code to be included.

```
outEmailFile.close();
```

_____

_____

_____

7. Explain the overall execution of the program.

_____

_____

You are now capable of creating and entering data into a sequential access file!

PROJECT 10-2:
Reading from a Sequential Access File

Now that you've created a sequential access file and have entered data into it, you need to be able to get the data out. This program will do just that! Once you've completed this project you will be able to write other programs that will enable you to read other sequential access files.

Step 1: Start Your Compiler

If your compiler is not already running, start it now.

Step 2: Type in Your Code

Type in your code as follows. Save it with the filename **Project 10-2.cpp**. Make sure you save your file often.

```cpp
// Project 10-2
// Reading a sequential file
// Programmer: <Your Name>

#include <iostream.h>
#include <fstream.h>
#include <iomanip.h>
#include <stdlib.h>

void outputRecord(const char *, const char *, const char *);

main()
{
   char fname[20];
   char lname[20];
   char email[30];

   ifstream inEmailFile("email.dat", ios::in);

   if (!inEmailFile)
   {
      cerr << "Could not open file!" << "\n";
      exit(1);
   }

   cout << "\nFirst Name" << setw(20) << "Last Name"
        << setw(36)  << "E-Mail Address\n";
   cout << "==========" << setw(20) << "=========" << setw(36) <<
```

249

```
"===============\n";

    while (inEmailFile >> fname >> lname >> email)
       outputRecord(fname, lname, email);

    cout << "\n";

    inEmailFile.close();

    return 0;
}


void outputRecord(const char *fname, const char *lname, const char *email)
{
    cout << setw(10) << fname << setw(20) << lname << setw(35) << email <<
"\n";
}
```

Step 3: Save Your Program

Once you have finished typing in your code, save your code one final time before compiling your program.

Step 4: Build, Link, Run

Enter the commands necessary to build, link, and run your program. If errors occur during any of these processes, check your code, correct any errors, and rerun the program.

This program should display the data you input in your file in Project 10-1. The program will open your **email.dat** file, print out column headers, and then work its way through the file, record by record, until all the data is displayed. The file is then closed and the program exits.

Step 5: Review Your Code

Now that your program has run successfully, review your code with your classmates and teacher to make sure you have a strong understanding of the techniques used in this program.

1. Explain why each of the four header files was required to be included.

_____

_____

2. Explain the following function prototype.

```
void outputRecord(const char *, const char *, const char *);
```

_____

_____

_____

3. Explain the following line of code.

```
ifstream inEmailFile("email.dat", ios::in);
```

_____

250

4. Explain the following block of code.

```
if (!inEmailFile)
{
   cerr << "Could not open file!" << "\n";
   exit(1);
}
```

5. Explain the following block of code.

```
while (inEmailFile >> fname >> lname >> email)
   outputRecord(fname, lname, email);
```

6. Explain the following line of code. Explain why it is, or is not, necessary for this line of code to be included.

```
inEmailFile.close();
```

7. Explain the following function definition.

```
void outputRecord(const char *fname, const char *lname, const char *email)
{
   cout << setw(10) << fname << setw(20) << lname << setw(35) << email << "\n";
}
```

8. Explain the overall execution of this program.

As you have learned, the difference between random access and sequential access is that sequential access order is based on a record key field. Random access is based on "instant access." You no longer need to search through every record to find the one you want.

The first step is to create an empty random access file. Part of the advantage, although at times it will be a disadvantage, of random access files is that the records can all be made the same length. This is one way to know where each record is because they are all the same length. In this project you will create an empty random access file with records that are identical in length. You will be using your car structure from Lesson 8 as the data example for the next three projects.

Step 1: Start Your Compiler

If your compiler is not already running, start it now.

Step 2: Type in Your Code

Type in your code as follows. Save it with the filename **Project 10-3.cpp**. Make sure you save your file often.

```cpp
// Project 10-3
// Create random access file
// Programmer: <Your Name>

#include <iostream.h>
#include <fstream.h>
#include <stdlib.h>

struct Car {
    int number;
    int speed;
    int mpg;
    int fuel;
};

main()
{
    ofstream outCar("car.dat", ios::out);

    if (!outCar)
    {
        cerr << "Could not create file!\n";
        exit(1);
    }

    Car EmptyCar = {0, 0, 0, 0};

    for (int ctr = 0; ctr < 50; ctr++)
        outCar.write(
            reinterpret_cast<const char *>(&EmptyCar),
```

```
            sizeof(EmptyCar));

    return 0;
}
```

Step 3: Save Your Program

Once you have finished typing in your code, save your code one final time before compiling your program.

Step 4: Build, Link, Run

Enter the commands necessary to build and link your program. If errors occur during any of these processes, check your code, correct any errors, and relink the program.

    The only way you will know that this program executed properly is to open the directory/folder in which your programs are stored. You should see a file named **car.dat** in that directory/folder. If you open the file with Notepad, or another text editor, it will be empty.

Step 5: Review Your Code

Now that your program has run successfully, review your code with your classmates and teacher.

1. Explain why each of the three header files was required to be included.

_____

_____

2. What is the purpose of the following block of code?

```
ofstream outCar("car.dat", ios::out);
```

_____

_____

3. Explain the following block of code.

```
if (!outCar)
{
   cerr << "Could not create file!\n";
   exit(1);
}
```

_____

_____

4. Explain the following line of code.

```
Car EmptyCar = {0, 0, 0, 0};
```

_____

_____

5. Explain the following block of code.

```
for (int ctr = 0; ctr < 50; ctr++)
   outCar.write(
      reinterpret_cast<const char *>(&EmptyCar),
      sizeof(EmptyCar));
```

_____

_____

_____

_____

_____

6. Explain the overall execution of the program.

_____

_____

_____

_____

This is the first step in using random access files. Now you'll learn how to input data to these random access files.

PROJECT 10-4:
Input Data to a Random Access File

Using the same car structure, with a minor modification, you will prompt the user for the data you need. Now when you open the **car.dat** file, it will not be empty. However, depending on how you enter the car information you may need to look through the file for it since it will not be in a sequential order.

You will use this program as a simple car dealer's inventory program. The user will be prompted to enter a car number, then the speed it travels, the miles per gallon it gets, and the amount of gas in the tank. When finished, the user will let the program know by entering 0.

One small item to pay attention to—the data you are entering does not need to be input in order. You can enter any car as long as it's between the "inventory numbers" you assigned as input ranges. The benefit of this is that you can simply input the car data in any order. An additional benefit will be shown in the next project.

Step 1: Start Your Compiler

If your compiler is not already running, start it now.

Step 2: Type in Your Code

Type in your code as follows. Save it with the filename **Project 10-4.cpp**. Make sure you save your file often.

```
// Project 10-4
// Input data to a random access file
// Programmer: <Your Name>

#include <iostream.h>
#include <iomanip.h>
#include <fstream.h>
#include <stdlib.h>

struct Car {
   int number;
   int speed;
   int mpg;
   int fuel;
};

main()
{
   Car InventoryCar;

   ofstream outCar("car.dat", ios::ate);

   if (!outCar)
   {
      cerr << "Could not open file!\n";
      exit(1);
   }

   cout << "Enter number of car.\n";
   cout << "(Number should be from 1 to 50. To end input, enter 0.): ";

   cin >> InventoryCar.number;

   while (InventoryCar.number > 0 && InventoryCar.number <= 50)
   {
      cout << "Enter Speed, Miles Per Gallon, and Fuel\n";
      cout << "Enter data: ";
      cin >> InventoryCar.speed >> InventoryCar.mpg >> InventoryCar.fuel;

      outCar.seekp((InventoryCar.number - 1) * sizeof(Car));

      outCar.write(reinterpret_cast<const char *>(&InventoryCar),
sizeof(Car));

      cout << "Enter number of car: ";
      cin >> InventoryCar.number;
   }

   return 0;
}
```

Step 3: Save Your Program

When you have completed typing the code, save your program once more before moving on to the next step.

Step 4: Build, Link, Run

Enter the commands necessary to build, link, and run your program. If errors occur during any of these processes, check your code, correct any errors, and rerun the program.

Remember to save your program any time you make changes!

Your program should *not* visibly work any different. Anything that happens with this program so far is happening behind the scenes as it builds the file. The difference between this project and the last one is that there is now data in the **car.dat** file. It may not be readable, but it is there! If you open your car.dat file with a text editor you will see some data.

Step 5: Explain Your Code

Review your code with your classmates and teacher. Concentrate on the lines of code that are shown below.

1. Explain the following line of code.

```
ofstream outCar("car.dat", ios::ate);
```

_____

_____

2. Explain the following block of code.

```
cout << "Enter number of car.\n";
cout << "(Number should be from 1 to 50. To end input, enter 0.): ";

cin >> InventoryCar.number;
```

_____

_____

_____

3. Explain the following block of code.

```
while (InventoryCar.number > 0 && InventoryCar.number <= 50)
{
    cout << "Enter Speed, Miles Per Gallon, and Fuel\n";
    cout << "Enter data: ";
    cin >> InventoryCar.speed >> InventoryCar.mpg >> InventoryCar.fuel;
```

_____

_____

_____

4. Explain the following line of code.

```
outCar.seekp((InventoryCar.number - 1) * sizeof(Car));
```

_____

_____

_____

_____

_____

5. Explain the following line of code.

```
outCar.write(reinterpret_cast<const char *>(&InventoryCar), sizeof(Car));
```

_____

_____

6. Why are the following lines of code repeated?

```
    cout << "Enter number of car: ";
    cin >> InventoryCar.number;
}
```

_____

_____

_____

7. Explain the overall execution of the program.

_____

_____

_____

_____

_____

_____

_____

_____

PROJECT 10-5:
Reading from a Random Access File

In this project, you will read the data that you have created. This particular program will only display the records that exist. If there are storage areas in the file that do not contain data, then they will not be displayed.

In the preceding project, an additional benefit of random input was mentioned. Pay attention to the output of your program and see if you notice the benefit. It will be discussed at the end of this project.

Step 1: Start Your Compiler

If your compiler is not already running, start it now.

Step 2: Type in Your Code

Type in your code as follows. Save it with the filename **Project 10-5.cpp**. Make sure you save your file often.

```
// Project 10-5
// Reading from random access file
// Programmer: <Your Name>
```

```
#include <iostream.h>
#include <iomanip.h>
#include <fstream.h>
#include <stdlib.h>

struct Car {
   int number;
   int speed;
   int mpg;
   int fuel;
};

void outputCar(ostream&, const Car &);

main()
{
   Car InventoryCar;

   ifstream inCar("car.dat", ios::in);

   if (!inCar)
   {
      cerr << "Could not open file!\n";
      exit(1);
   }

   cout << "Car Number" << setw(10) << "Speed" << setw(10) << "MPG" <<
setw(11) << "Fuel\n";
   cout << "==========" << setw(10) << "=====" << setw(10) << "===" <<
setw(11) << "====\n";

   inCar.read(reinterpret_cast<char *>(&InventoryCar),
      sizeof(Car));

   while (inCar && !inCar.eof())
   {
      if (InventoryCar.number != 0)
         outputCar(cout, InventoryCar);

      inCar.read(reinterpret_cast<char *>(&InventoryCar),
         sizeof(Car));
   }

   return 0;
}


void outputCar(ostream &output, const Car &c)
{
   output << setw(10) << c.number << setw(10) << c.speed
          << setw(10) << c.mpg << setw(10) << c.fuel << "\n";
}
```

Step 3: Save Your Program

Once you have finished typing in your code, save your code one final time before compiling your program.

258

Step 4: Build, Link, Run

Enter the commands necessary to build, link, and run your program. If errors occur during any of these processes, check your code, correct any errors, and rerun the program.

Your program should open the car.dat file, print column headings for the output, and then display all the records in the file that are not empty records.

Step 5: Review Your Code

Review your code with your classmates and teacher. Concentrate on the lines of code that are shown below.

1. Explain the following function prototype.

```
void outputCar(ostream&, const Car &);
```

_____

_____

_____

2. Explain the following line of code.

```
ifstream inCar("car.dat", ios::in);
```

_____

_____

3. Explain the following line of code.

```
inCar.read(reinterpret_cast<char *>(&InventoryCar),
    sizeof(Car));
```

_____

_____

4. Explain the following block of code.

```
while (inCar && !inCar.eof())
{
   if (InventoryCar.number != 0)
      outputCar(cout, InventoryCar);

   inCar.read(reinterpret_cast<char *>(&InventoryCar),
      sizeof(Car));
}
```

_____

_____

_____

_____

_____

_____

5. Explain the following function definition.

```
void outputCar(ostream &output, const Car &c)
{
    output << setw(10) << c.number << setw(10) << c.speed
           << setw(10) << c.mpg << setw(10) << c.fuel << "\n";
}
```

_____

_____

_____

6. Explain the overall program execution.

_____

7. Explain the additional benefit associated with the random input of data.

_____

_____

You are now capable of creating sequential access and random access files. You should now possess the abilities to become a productive C++ programmer. But, remember that being a good programmer takes hard work, persistence, and a continuing curiosity about the intricacies of the language.

Summary

It's not enough to input data, manipulate it, and then display it. Data needs to be stored for future reference. That's why there is such a proliferation of databases.

In this lesson, you learned about two different file structures: Sequential access is that which is built around the key record field or the identifier of the record. Any additional information to be input to sequential files must be added at the end because there's no way to move the records around inside the file. Random access files, on the other hand, are created empty with record storage areas of identical length. Data can be input randomly or sequentially. However, random input is much easier because you do not need to spend time putting the data in order—the program does it for you. And, when you read the data, it is automatically sorted. This is a nice side benefit, plus it's a great deal quicker than a bubble sort.

This lesson is a culmination of everything you've learned in this book. You can perform many functions in your programs, you can manipulate data, create structures and classes, and now you can store it to _**permanent storage media**_. You have all the tools you need to be a successful entry-level C++ programmer!

LESSON 10 REVIEW QUESTIONS

SHORT ANSWER

Define the following in the space provided.

1. Sequential access

_____

2. Random access

_____

_____

3. Field

_____

4. Record

_____

5. File

_____

6. Database

_____

7. Record key field

_____

8. Append

_____

9. Instant access

_____

10. Permanent storage media

_____

_____

WRITTEN QUESTIONS

Write your answers to the following questions in the space provided.

1. Explain how data is organized within a file.

_____

_____

2. Explain the difference between sequential access and random access.

_____

_____

_____

3. How can you make sure that files, similar to the ones in the projects in this lesson, have been created?

_____

_____

4. How is the size of an empty random access file calculated by the system?

_____

_____

_____

_____

_____

_____

5. Explain why an empty random access file has a size, but an empty text file has no size.

_____

_____

_____

TESTING YOUR SKILLS

⏱ **Estimated Time:**

Application 10-1 1 hour
Application 10-2 1 hour
Application 10-3 1 hour

APPLICATION 10-1 B

Using Project 10-1 as an example, create a sequential file that will contain the class name and grade for all classes you have taken this year. Code your program so that numeric grades are entered. Letter grades may conflict with the EOF character. Save your file as **App10-1.cpp**.

APPLICATION 10-2 I

Using Project 10-2 as an example, create a program that will read the data from your class name and grade file. Save your file as **App10-2.cpp**.

APPLICATION 10-3 I

1. You will append records to your email.dat file created in Project 10-1. Open your **Project 10-1.cpp** file and then save it as **App10-3.cpp**.

2. You will need to modify your code in two places to append records to the end of the file. One modification will actually allow the modification to take place. The other will modify the error regarding not being able to access the file.

3. Test your modifications by executing Project 10-2.

CRITICAL THINKING A

⏱ **Estimated Time: 2–3 hours**

Create data files using any project that you completed in this book that required the user to input data. For example, saving the payroll calculations for each employee from Lesson 6, or saving the Person class in Project 9-1. Or, you can even create entirely new programs that request information from the user that is important to you—record collections, stamp collections, etc. Remember that users typically store information for later use. This is the basis of database creation and manipulation. Use your abilities to save the data from the programs that are meaningful to you.

Be aware of the fact that some files will lend themselves to a sequential structure and others will lend themselves to a random access structure. Experiment to see which structure is most appropriate.

INDEX

Addresses, types of, 163
Aggregate data type, 191, 213
Appending, 245
Arithmetic operators, 47
Array(s), 163
   declaring size of, 191
   designing, 192–193
   double subscript, 195–198
   initializing, from user input,
     172–174
   multiple subscript, 191
   simple, 164–167
   single subscript, 192–195
   size of, using constant variable to
     set, 174–176
   two, compiling survey results
     using, 176–179
Array output, formatting, 167–169
Ascending order, 164
Attributes, 205

Base class pointer, 230
Binary search, 182
Bubble sort, 179–182
Build, link
   stopping after, 40
   and run, 5
   See also Rebuild, link, run

Calculations
   performing, vs. storing values,
     35–36, 58
   proper use of variables in, 36
   purpose of, 35
Calling functions, 50
Checkbook balancing, 7–9
Class, 191, 205–208
   defining, 207
   derived, 225–230
   designing, 214–217, 235–237
   multiple instances of, 235–241
   simple, 214–221
Code
   adding comments to, 5–6, 38
   analyzing, 140
   calculations and, 36
   general outline of main (), 39, 41

organizing, into function, 36
printing, 66–68
reviewing, importance of, 4–5
See also Pseudocode
Code, creating
   for federal withholding function,
     147–148
   for medical insurance function,
     147–148
   for program structure, 132–135
Compiler, starting, 2–3
Concatenation, 46
Constant variable, 164
   to set array size, 174–176
Constructors and destructors,
   221–225
Control structures, 65
   repetition, 99
Conversion
   decimal to hexadecimal and octal,
     36–38
   distance, 2–7
   dollar to foreign currency, 41–43
   foreign currency, 38–40
   height, feet and inches to cen-
     timeters and meters, 44–46
Counter, 100

Data, finding, 40, 43
Database, 246
Data input, 24–29
   to random access file, 254–257
Data type, aggregate, 191
Decimal to hexadecimal and octal
   conversion, 36–38
DELETE menu item, creating inter-
   face screen for, 33
Derived classes, 225–230
Descending order, 164
Destructors, constructors and,
   221–225
Distance conversions, 2–7
Distributed processing, 58
Do/while structure, 99–100
   typing code for, 103
Dot operator/member access
   operator, 191

Element, 163
Encapsulation, 221
End of file. *See* EOF
End users, 13
EOF, 119–124
Escape characters, 17–18
Explicit address, 163
Extensions
   .cpp, 4, 7
   .h, 56

Field, 246
   record key, 245
File, 246
   sequential access, reading from,
     249–251
   See also Header file, Random ac-
     cess file, Sequential access file
Flowchart, 41
For structure, 99–100
   typing code for, 101
Foreign currency conversions, 38–40
Formatting, array output, 167–169
Function(s), 44, 50–52
   additional, 29, 147–151
   copying, 79
   hoursEntry, 139–147
   multiple, 52–56
   organizing code into, 36
   virtual, 230–234
   void, 75
Functionality, 65
Function definition, 50
Function prototype, 50

Header file, 37, 56–57
Height conversion, feet and inches to
   centimeters and meters, 44–46
Hex manipulator, 37–38
Hours, entry function, 139–147

If statements, 65
If/else statements, 65
   nested, 69
If/else structure, 65, 69–71
   with existing programs, 83–85
   and switch, 86

Implementation, 213
Implicit address, 163
Increment, 100
Infrastructures, 58
Initializing, array, from user input,
        172–174
Instance(s), 198, 202
        multiple, of class, 235–241
Interest
        compound, 115–119
        short-term/simple, 47–49
Interface, 213
        See also Intuitive interface, User
            interface
Intuitive interface, 14
Invoking functions, 50

Linear search, 182
Linking, 198
        See also Build, link and run
Loan, short-term/simple interest, 47–49
Loop, 80, 99
        for additional employees, 152–157

Main (), coding general outline of, 39,
        41
Manipulators, 36
Member functions, 205
Members, 198
Memory address, 163
Menu
        branching off, 75–83
        simple, with while repetition struc-
            ture, 105–108
Menu aesthetics, 20–23
Menu choices, 14–20
        additional functions, 29
        limitations, 23–24
Menu review, simple, 66–71
Methods, 205
MODIFY menu item, creating interface
        screen for, 33
Multiple selection, 86–91

Nested if/else statements, 69
New line (\n), 18

Object-oriented programming, 26, 213
Objects, 26, 36, 191
Oct manipulator, 37–38

Off-by-one errors, 164
Operators
        arithmetic, 47
        precedence among order of, 36
        stream insertion, 46
Output, 17–20

Payroll program, 130–139
Permanent storage media, 260
Pointer, 163, 169–171
        base class, 230
Post-increment, 103
Precedence, 47
        among order of operators, 36
Preincrement, 103
Preprocessor command line, 37
Program
        analyzing, to determine correctness,
            36
        existing, if/else structure with,
            83–85
        payroll, 130–139
        saving, 3–4
        testing, with Add a New Record
            screen, 80
        See also Code, Object-oriented pro-
            gramming
Program structure
        creating code for, 132–135
        designing, 130–132
Pseudocode, 41

Random access file, 245
        creating empty, 252–254
        inputting data to, 254–257
        reading from, 257–260
Rebuild, link, run, 7, 19, 38
Record, 246
Record key field, 245
Reference, 163, 230
Repetition control structures, 65, 99
        designing, 116–117
Repetition overview, 100–105
Run command. *See* Build, link and run
        See also Build, link and run

Saving, importance of, 3–4
Screen
        clearing, 80
        repeating, 108

Searching, 182–185
Selection, multiple, 86–91
Sequence control structures, 65, 99
Sequential access file, 245
        reading from, 249–251
Sorting, 164
        See also Bubble sort
Storing values, calculations vs., 35–36,
        58
Struct, 191
Structure member, 202
Structures, 191, 198–202
        self-referential, 202–205
        See also Control structures,
            Do/while structure, For struc-
            ture, If/else structure, Program
            structure, Repetition control
            structures, Selection control
            structures, Sequence control
            structures, Switch structure
Subscript, 163
        double, 195–198
        multiple, 191
        single, 192–195
Survey results, compiling, using two
        arrays, 176–179
Switch structure, 65, 71–74
        and if/else, 86
System capabilities, 58

User-defined type, 213
User-friendly, 13
User interaction, 14
        relating calculations to, 36
User interface, 13
        integrating checks into, 14
        See also Intuitive interface

Variables
        proper use of, in calculations, 36
        See also Constant variable
VIEW/PRINT menu item, creating
        interface screen for, 33
Virtual functions, 230–234
Void function, 75

While structure, 80–83, 99–100
        simple menu with, 105–108
        typing code for, 102